YESTERDAY, TODAY, AND TOMORROW
THE FARMER TAKES A HAND

D1086275

By Marquis Childs

Non-fiction:

Sweden: the Middle Way
This Is Democracy
Sweden's Labor Courts
Washington Calling
I Write from Washington
They Hate Roosevelt
Eisenhower, Captive Hero
The Ragged Edge
The Farmer Takes a Hand
Witness to Power

Fiction:

The Cabin
The Peacemakers
Taint of Innocence

Credits:
Production Editor, Erma Angevine
Cover and Typography Design, Jane Crawford
Cover Photograph, Charles O'Rear, USDA
Index, Richard A. Pence
Printed by McArdle Book Division

Yesterday Today and Tomorrow
The Farmer Takes a Hand

by Marquis W. Childs

This book includes the complete 1952
edition of The Farmer Takes a Hand, a new
foreword to the combined editions, and
Yesterday, Today, and Tomorrow, a supplement
updating the original edition.

Published by the
National Rural Electric Cooperative Association
1800 Massachusetts Avenue NW
Washington, D. C. 20036

1980

This book is dedicated to Clyde T. Ellis,
a mover and shaker who gave so much through
the years to rural electrification as it transformed
a way of life on the farms of America.

ACKNOWLEDGEMENTS

As with the initial volume so many people have helped me in writing the supplement that it would be impossible to name them all in a short space. My warmest thanks go once again to William S. Roberts of NRECA. Many members of the NRECA staff have been generous with their time in providing background and counsel. My thanks go especially to J. C. Brown and Robert Nelson whose long involvement in rural electrification and NRECA made them invaluable counselors. Out in the country I have had help from many veterans of the rapidly developing new phase of the growth of rural electric power. I would like to single out Gus Norwood of the Pacific Northwest for the generous guidance he provided a visitor. The staff of the REA in Washington has been unfailingly helpful.

CONTENTS

Foreword

The Farmer Takes a Hand

Yesterday, Today, and Tomorrow

FOREWORD

T HE story of rural electrification from 1935 to 1952 has some resemblance to an early melodrama in which the good and the bad contend in clearly defined opposition. For the purposes of that story, it was the dark and the light that were in conflict. To be sure there were shades of gray, yet time after time it was the co-ops contesting for the right to furnish electricity to even the remotest farm areas against the investor owned utilities.

That was a stirring chapter in the nation's life, and as I went from one region to another at that time I had a sense of growth and joy and reward in that growth. I was reminded of my native Iowa when the contrast between the city and the small town dweller was in such dramatic contrast to the family on the farm. That was changing and changing rapidly. Whether in regional meetings in Vermont or in Arkansas, members turned out by the hundreds to hail their achievements and plan for more to come. Their confidence and their enthusiasm were contagious.

Even in that beginning phase numbers could measure the benefits. The number of tenant farms declined as farmers with a new addition of light and power stayed on the land. Other factors such as paved roads were part of this. But it was the transformation in the home, the barns, the milking parlor that more than anything else changed the outlook for a whole generation of farm folks. The transformation was made possible for the most part by distribution co-ops.

The changes that have taken place since that first phase of rapid growth are amazing and fundamental and so, it seems to me, is the changed relationship between the co-ops and the investor owned utilities. In instance after instance they have worked together to create jointly owned sources of electricity. One reason is the ever increasing demand for energy and the capacity of the co-ops to obtain loans for generation and transmission. The G and Ts that have come into being have made a sizeable increase in the total power supply when it was most needed. This coincided with the problems that investor owned utilities often encountered in raising capital for new power resources.

Another and equally important reason was the coming of the nuclear age. The National Rural Electric Co-operative Association had boldly faced the necessity of power from the peaceful atom if the total supply of energy was to be sufficient to sustain the growing economy. But the demand was for billions rather than hundreds of millions as the cost of the new technology advanced. Repeatedly the burden has been shared. This has contributed appreciably to raising the output of power in region after region and, despite Three Mile Island and the strictures contained in the reports of the presidential commission on the need for far more stringent safeguards, it is certain to increase. Twenty G and T co-operatives have thus far obtained loans for sharing in nuclear plants, with percentages of ownership varying from 56 to .5 per cent. Most are to come on line in the early '80s.

However essential the sharing has been it raises a vital question. The co-operative concept was the basis of the REA. It was the essential ingredient of the co-ops that spread with such zeal and enthusiasm in the early phase. If this concept is obscured and the big G and T co-ops appear as merely part of the utility industry, the political consequences must be reckoned with. A more conservative Congress bent on economy in government could question loans at interest rates amounting to a subsidy. The cost of the REA itself, with the memory of President Nixon's abrupt effort to strangle the program, might be a target.

With the widespread support NRECA has in Congress this may be merely to borrow future trouble that may never materialize. Nevertheless it seems to me imperative that the co-operative concept be sustained. As when I did my first survey of the electrification program, the concept of co-operation seems to have been almost as important in contributing to the health and wellbeing of American life as the physical transformation. It will not be easy. In areas where suburbs have encroached on farm land and suburban households have become co-op members, the suburbanites are interested in low cost power but the concept behind their membership is likely to mean little.

Determined effort and dedication are necessary. It can be done. I cite the example of James Grahl presiding over Basin Electric with its eight-state coverage and its complicated power system. He nevertheless manages to infuse a sense of common purpose into a multi-million membership. Another example is Carl Turner of New Mexico bringing a personal stewardship to his far flung province.

In the short space of a supplement to the original volume I have been able to give only a glimpse of some of the more significant developments in the later phase of rural electrification. So much that is varied and important is happening in region after region; in Missouri, Pennsylvania, Wisconsin. I only wish that I had had time and more space to include much more of the story. Another book may be in order to tell at least a larger part of the new phase of an exciting development that is transforming the land.

Marquis W. Childs
Washington, D.C.

The Farmer
Takes a Hand

Chapter One
REVOLT ON THE FARM

MEASURED against the ordinary flow of events, twenty years is a short span of time. But the two decades we have just come through have been crowded with history on the grand scale, and as a consequence, a great deal that has happened has been obliterated. There enters here, too, one of the curious things about human memory. We want to forget what was threatening, menacing, promising the destruction of our whole way of life.

Some of the results of the upheaval that began in 1932 are obvious enough. Others are less apparent in the turmoil and the rush and conflict that have characterized the intervening years. If any of the changes that have taken place can truly be described as revolutionary, it is the transformation that has occurred on the farms in this country. Here a way of life has been profoundly altered, and yet those of us who live in the cities have been more or less unaware of how extensive the alteration has been. There are many reasons for the change that has taken place. But the key may well be the extension of electric power to American farms. In 1932 only ten per cent of all farms had electricity. Today approximately ninety per cent have electric service delivered by distribution line from central stations.

What happened in 1931 and 1932, and, perhaps even more important, what led up to those years, seem to us today like events that occurred in a remote period of history. We can scarcely believe that it was only yesterday. The statistics are available. Wheat was selling for thirty-seven cents a bushel. Hogs on the Chicago market brought $2.68 a hundredweight in the fall of 1932. Corn was being burned for fuel because it was cheaper than coal. Just how many millions were out of work in the cities or employed only part time no one really knew. But it could scarcely have been less than fifteen million, and it may have been as high as twenty million. The traditional relief agencies could carry only a small fraction of the load.

But the statistics fail to recreate the atmosphere of that time and particularly the angry hum of revolt that came from the farm belt. It was not less than that. Here were boiling up resentments and frustrations arising from a conviction of ancient wrong.

On the roads in Minnesota were farmers armed with shotguns. In the futile hope of driving prices up, they formed picket lines in a desperate attempt to prevent produce from reaching the market. In some instances violence grew out of these picket lines. Milk ran in the ditches along the road side in Wisconsin and Minnesota. In Wisconsin a cheese factory was dynamited by angry farmers. Local sheriffs were either powerless against this grass-root rebellion or they were secretly in sympathy with it. When they tried to intervene, in rare instances, they were usually disarmed and sent back to town. The National Guard might have broken these picket lines. But politically conscious governors knew better than to attempt any such drastic action.

One out of every four farms was sold for debts and taxes. Insurance companies enormously increased their holdings of farm lands. In Iowa, the richest of our farm states, a quarter of all farms went through forced sales.

In the rebellion that came after 1930 the farmers were not without leaders daring enough and fearless enough to meet force with force. At many a forced sale farmers with their guns stood about the courthouse door. The farm was bid in for one dollar and other valuable considerations and then it was turned back to its original owner. Here again the sheriffs were powerless or in sympathy with the rebels.

One of the leaders remarkably well cast in a Robespierre role was Milo Reno. Reno knew the history of the Grange and Populist movements. In a sense he was the inheritor of those other wild-eyed men, those sons of the wild jackass, who had in an earlier time of ruinous farm prices and corresponding farm rebellion tried to make articulate the angry discontent of the prairies. With his stiff, stalked hair and steel-rimmed spectacles, looking fierce as an old eagle, Reno traveled about the countryside organizing farmers to petition state and national governments for relief payments and a moratorium on debts. With his harsh, jerky gestures and his rasping voice, he preached a farm holiday, equality of opportunity for the farmer, an end of injustice and the slavery of Wall Street. A reporter of the time saw Reno drive ". . . up in a storm of dust and wind to a remote country schoolhouse and light into the bankers and bloodsuckers under a row of swinging lanterns with a prairie wind sniffling and sucking at the corner of the roof . . ."

But the farmers of that time needed little incitation. It was hard to realize that these angry men had up until recently thought of themselves as Republicans, as conservatives, as the backbone of America. When on several occasions their leaders were arrested, these same conservatives, these farmers, these Republicans, advanced in a determined crowd on the jail. Quickly the prisoners would be released. While this revolt on the farm may have come as a shock and a surprise to some, it had been brewing for a long time. The sense of injustice, the deep resentment, went a long way into the American past. Populists, representing a merger of the Grange movement with the Farmers' Alliance, polled more than a million votes in the election of 1892. The high tariff protecting the manufacturer who made everything the farmer had to buy was the root of all evil, as innumerable orators proclaimed at Grange picnics and political rallies. The farmer sold low and bought dear. The manufacturer, the bloated character with the dollar signs on his frock coat as portrayed in Hearst cartoons, lived under a protective umbrella provided by the government. The farmer who took his grain and his hogs to market was a lonely figure, subject not only to the rise and fall in prices on the world market but to the wicked manipulations of speculators in the East.

For generations this had been the theme that brought ringing applause from farm audiences. On this theme William Jennings Bryan, the boy orator from the Platte, rang many changes when, for the first time in American history, he was chosen by a major political party for a third attempt to win the presidency. In Wisconsin "Fighting Bob" La Follette preached something of the same doctrine against inequity and injustice, helping in this way to launch the Wisconsin experiment in social reform. It was an inherent part of the American political pattern, as American industry was beginning to develop new and unrivaled productivity. The farmer came to believe that this productivity, and the profits that grew out of it, were largely at his expense.

During World War I he had a brief taste of prosperity. The inflated prices of the war encouraged the disastrous land boom of 1919 and 1920. For a short time farm land brought fantastic prices—$500 and $600 an acre in Iowa and in surrounding states. This was the millennium.

But the drop came with sickening swiftness. Farm prices collapsed in 1921. The American farmer had enormously expanded his crop acreage to meet the demand for food during the war. He now found himself selling in a market glutted by a huge world supply; a disastrous oversupply, the economists said. It was a trap in which the farmer each year seemed to become more deeply and more ruinously involved. The more he produced, the bigger the supply and hence the smaller his return.

What made this trap all the more cruel was that everything the farmer bought each year cost him more: his cultivator, his hay wagon, barbed wire for his fences, even the kerosene for the lamps in his house. There just seemed to be no way out even though a lot of people talked about what should be done or even sometimes what could be done.

There were friends of the farmer in Washington who, as the pit grew deeper, thought that government should take some action to help the farmer out of the trap. One of them was Senator Charles McNary of Oregon, a Republican, who felt strongly that farmers were getting a raw deal and who believed that something should be done about it. McNary worked with farm leaders and with Representative Haugen of Iowa, also a Republican, to frame a bill which would bring belated justice to the unhappy son of the soil. The McNary-Haugen Bill, would have established a fund with federal aid to permit the farmer to dump his staples, when they were judged in surplus, on the foreign market. Thereby higher prices would result for the supplies that remained in the home market. This was obviously a compensation for the tariff act: another kind of government umbrella, held in this instance over the defenseless farmer.

Twice Congress passed the McNary-Haugen Bill, and twice it was vetoed, once by Calvin Coolidge and once by Herbert Hoover. They held that it was un-American. These vetoes produced political consequences of a most far-reaching nature. It is quite possible that they contributed more than any other single factor to the five Democratic victories which followed.

The stock-market crash of 1929 signaled the end for the farmer. Five-cent cotton and thirty-seven-cent wheat were disaster, stark and unmitigated. Farmers' automobiles disappeared from the roads. Farm children began to drop out of schools and colleges because there was no money to keep them there even on a self-help basis.

This was, of course, only one aspect of the country's plight. Thousands of unemployed men and women wandered the streets of the cities seeking in vain for work, combing the garbage pails for a few scraps to eat. The cities themselves were bankrupt. Chicago could not even pay its employees. As Arthur Krock was to write in the New York *Times* in retrospect of this period, civic leaders feared the "honest violence of the starving," because with no work, with no prospect of any, with factories shut down but with a family to feed and shelter, the "social brink" had been reached.

In this climate of fear and desperation demagogues flourished. Huey Long, the Kingfish from Louisiana, was reaching the height of his power as the depression deepened. The appeal of his Share-the-Wealth program, which the Kingfish presented in the framework of his own earthy humor, attracted millions. "If we do not break up the concentration of wealth in the hands of a few, it will not be possible to feed and clothe the American people," Long told one huge audience after another.

In Detroit a Roman Catholic priest, Father Charles Coughlin, had built up a vast following with a radio program that savored of populism and seemed to offer relief from the obvious defects of the existing financial system. The radio priest called for a National Union of Social Justice pledged to fight for a living annual wage, the nationalization of banking and currency and natural resources.

Another leader with a powerful public appeal was Dr. Francis Townsend. The good doctor had spent his life practicing medicine among the poor farmers of South Dakota in the Black Hills. When he was middle-aged, Townsend moved with his family to Long Beach, California, where he managed to weather out the depression. One day while looking out of his comfortable house, Dr. Townsend saw three old women searching through a garbage pail for food. This, he was often to say later, launched him on his crusade for the aged poor. By 1935 the Townsend movement had three million members, and ten million other followers were said to hold the political balance in eleven states.

But strong as the forces were that threw demagogues up to the top, they lacked the unrelenting determiniation, the steady irresistible drive that had grown up through the years on the farm. This could have come only out of a deep-seated sense of wrong, a resentment accumulating in good seasons as well as bad, as the farmer felt himself deprived, with the aid of something like a conspiracy managed in the East, of all the benefits of modern life. While only ten per cent of farm homes had electricity, in the cities and towns the percentage was seventy per cent. The electric power industry had told the farmer in almost so many words that it was too costly to furnish him power except in the rare instances where farms were near towns. The utilities had said that he had little use for electricity in any event. The farmer felt this was part of an easy conviction that his lot was inevitably a hard one with the luxuries of the city beyond his reach.

It was partly against this that the farmer was revolting. His leaders were convinced that he could have benefits such as electric power. Nor were these the radicals and the hotheads. Stout conservatives from the South like Ed O'Neal of the American Farm Bureau Federation led the way in the early days of the New Deal in demanding rural electrification. Given the circumstances, this demand was irresistible.

Along with the whole far-reaching program of subsidies, parity prices, and soil conservation, electricity now has come to the farm. It has come in typically American fashion through a working relationship between Government, farm leaders, traditional co-operatives, and commercial business. Sometimes private enterprise has co-operated willingly, sometimes reluctantly. But whatever the attitude, it is nevertheless clearly demonstrable that the power load of the private utilities and, likewise, the profits of private utilities have been greatly increased by the transformation worked on the American farm. In 1951 the commercial utility companies sold $43,000,000 worth of power to the Rural Electrification Administration borrowers. Private enterprise has built the refrigerators, the dairy equipment, the hay dryers, the lighting systems, the food freezers, the toasters and washing machines that are found on farms across the land; and this is to say nothing of the generators and other facilities necessary to produce the increased power for distribution to America's farm families.

Propaganda has never ceased to try to make rural electrification as it had been carried out with the help of government financing sound like something dangerous and radical, socialist or even communist. Actually it can be shown that virtually no federal subsidy at all has gone into this pay-as-you-go system. But either with or without government subsidy the farmer had not been frightened by this talk. Through the years he has come to regard the high tariff itself as a form of subsidy to the American manufacturer, and a subsidy, moreover, that he himself is paying. When the lights are turned on for the first time in the farm kitchen and in the cow barn, that is something tangible and real, an achievement which the farmer believes is his own and which no politican can take away from him.

Chapter Two
THE BEGINNING

IN THE YEARS after 1932 a great many forces converged to light up the farms of America. First and foremost, of course, was the demand that welled up out of farm homes in every part of the country. But that demand had existed for a long time and nothing had come of it. The farmer had been told by all sorts and conditions of experts in the power industry that it was out of the question, impractical, unjustified on any sound economic basis.

It was not that the private power industry had been unaware of this demand. A great deal of serious consideration had, in fact, been given to it. The electric industry was just thirty years old in 1911, but already progressive power company executives had become conscious of the potential farm market. In those years, however, the industry was still absorbed in electrifying the cities, in perfecting the rather primitive generating equipment of the day, and in trying to develop an industrial market. In World War I the entire resources of the industry were absorbed in supplying power to the manufacturers.

When the war ended, discussion began again over what could be done to bring power lines to the farms. In some areas developments already started seemed to point the way. In California the irrigation of large tracts of land in reclamation projects which developed electric power as a by-product made it profitable for the utility companies to go into country districts. Here and there in the Midwest and in the Northwest farmers had formed electric cooperatives to help themselves get power.

But these developments were exceptions in a picture that was generally dark. As the demand from the farms grew steadily after 1918, utility executives found themselves in a somewhat embarrassing situation. Grover Neff, then president of the Wisconsin Power Company, said, "This is indeed an unusual situation. The farmer, a user of power, is trying to force the utility, a seller of power, to sell him the product it has for sale." The pressure grew more insistent, coming from organized farm groups and from congressmen from rural states. There were utility executives, too, who realized that this was a responsibility which they could not ignore.

In 1923 the National Electric Light Association, forerunner of the Edison Electric Institute, organized the Committee on the Relation of Electricity to Agriculture. This committee, which came to be known as CREA, brought together farm groups, government bureaus, and equipment manufacturers to study the potential uses of electricity on the farm and to determine whether a profitable farm market could be built up. Although CREA was largely financed by the private power industry, all of the groups that worked with the committee donated large amounts of time and money. When the committee began its studies in 1923, all its members believed that rural electrification was the job of the private power industry. Eleven years later the farm organizations and many in Congress and in the federal Government despaired of anything ever being done through private enterprise.

It was not that CREA failed to function. A great deal of useful information came out of its work. A major experimental project was established at Red Wing, Minnesota, to demonstrate how electricity could better farm life.

The rolling countryside around Red Wing, sweeping back from the Mississippi River, a country of prosperous dairy farms, was in many ways ideally suited to such an experiment. The project was on a limited scale, consisting of a six-mile snake line serving perhaps twenty farm homes. The objective was to find out how electricity could be used and whether the farmer could afford to pay the rates a private power company would have to charge. The local utility company, the state university, and twenty nationally known manufacturers joined forces to conduct exhaustive tests.

Ten farmhouses were equipped with practically every electric appliance then existing. Electricity was installed in the farmers' barns, chicken houses, and milk sheds. Electric motors were installed for dehydrating hay. An electric motor saw for cutting wood replaced the two-man handsaw. An electric pump brought running water into the houses. Separate meters recorded the amount of electricity used by all of these devices. And at the same time the farmer kept a careful check on his operating costs. As the experiment progressed, electric bills rose sharply. But at the same time the individual farmer found his operating costs decreasing. Electricity was saving months of labor each year and thus the farmer was able to use his energy profitably at other jobs. Quite apart from these statistics, it was abundantly clear that life on the experimental farms was happier and healthier. The whole level of farm living had been raised by abolishing some of the back-breaking tasks of farm life.

The Cady, the Eckbald, the Nelson, and the Bryan families, who took part in the Red Wing project, learned that they must not only use electricity to light their houses, but they must put it to work everywhere on the farm. They learned that it was not a question of whether the farmer could afford to use some electrical equipment. The farmers in the Red Wing experiment discovered that they and the power companies got a greater return the more electricity each farm employed. The rate of return went up steadily as more and more uses were made of the current that had been brought from the city.

Across the country state committees were formed to study the relationship of electricity to agriculture. In many instances these committees worked energetically to apply electricity to special conditions of the farming countryside. A great educational campaign was carried on to show the farmer how he could put electricity to work.

There was a certain irony in all this activity. The problem was no longer what to use electricity for but how to get it. The colleges, the agricultural extension schools, the Rockefeller Foundation, the Boyce Thompson Institute, and manufacturers such as Westinghouse, General Electric, and Worthington had developed new ways and had improved old ones for applying electric power to farm work. Experiments ranged all the way from using electric energy to burn a field clear of stumps and to drying tons of hay to a Detroit farmer's discovery that cows like to have radio music in the barn while they are being milked. Methods for drying grain and foods were developed. Electric brooders for chicks were perfected and hotbeds for growing seedlings were wired for electric current. It was shown that electric heat could help farmers keep their bees from being winter-killed in very cold climates. Improved water pumps were developed that lifted thousands of gallons a minute to irrigate the arid lands of the West. During this same period engineers were working to reduce the cost of building power lines. Cedar, pine, cement, and steel poles were being experimented with. Transformers were placed on the market that were at the same time cheaper and better adapted to the fluctuating demands of rural lines.

Out of the work of CREA came many reports showing in detail that rural electrification was practical. But still the electric industry failed to act. Even after reading the reports of the committee they had created, the utility companies thought of the farmer as a small and unimportant domestic consumer of electricity. The farm market was considered too limited to warrant the investment needed to build costly rural power lines. When they were told that perhaps they had a social responsibility to bring electricity to the farms, power company spokesmen retorted tartly that the utility industry was not a charitable institution. If the farmer wanted electricity on his farm, said the power companies, or most of them, then he must make sacrifices in order to pay for it. As CREA had shown, only a few farmers could afford to pay the two or three or five or six thousand dollars that it cost to get "hooked up."

What the utility companies seemingly did not understand was that the problem went much deeper than this. Even if the farmer could pay several thousand dollars to bring the electric line to his farm, he could not afford the high price charged for electric power. That was the basic issue. The National Master of the Grange, Louis Taber, one of the most conservative of farm leaders, put it this way:

"The problem of lower rates will continue to be an issue until adjustments are made and there is a clearer understanding of the problems underlying the cost of manufacturing and transmitting electrical energy."

Taber and the other farm leaders were under no illusions about the state of the power industry. It was completely demoralized. As Taber put it, "We have made a great mistake in allowing power companies to pyramid stock values with every consolidation and combination. The amount of water pumped into some of these corporations approaches a scandal." The wild debauch of the power industry through the device of the holding company is one of the tragic chapters in the history of American private enterprise.

The system of the holding company was not bad in and of itself. Holding companies played an important part in the growth of the young electric light companies into one of America's largest industries. Thanks often to the excellent engineering and legal services they provided, they made possible economies that could have come only through centralized management.

But throughout the twenties the holding company became more and more the creature of financial exploiters who were only incidentally interested in the electric industry and its sound development for both service and profit. Operators like Samuel Insull, reaching out for more and more companies, gave little heed to the real function of the industry in which they had chosen to carry on their schemes of lurid high finance.

The production and distribution of electric power is almost in its very nature a monopoly. There can be little or none of the kind of competition that has been the dynamic of free enterprise in America. It is in this respect in striking contrast to the automobile industry, to cite only one example. The status of the power industry, both as a monopoly and as an essential public service, had long been recognized, with the necessity for public determination, through regulating bodies, of the rate to be charged to the consumer. Recognizing the monopolistic nature of the power industry, the advocates of publicly owned and developed power had for years been arguing the need for something more than regulation. In 1932 there were 1835 municipally owned power plants in existence, as one evidence of the public power movement.

Using the device of the holding company, the big-time operators had extended their domination over one utility company after another through the purchase of small but controlling amounts of the company's stock. Insull's Middlewest Corporation was the largest and the most fantastic of these pyramided holding companies. It controlled 152 subsidiaries which in turn controlled an additional 74 companies. The wild and reckless growth of these corporations led to an amazing conglomeration of properties, so weird and complex that often no one, least of all the financiers who had put them together, knew just what they did contain. For example, one company owned water, ice, coal, oil, real estate, and investment companies. There were utility holding companies operating farms, quarries, gas stations, parking lots, laundries and even a southern baseball team.

These holding companies were created by stock-market operators, insurance companies and banks, and in some instances by high-powered law firms. Those who directed these far-flung enterprises were remote from the companies that actually generated and distributed electricity in the towns and cities of America. They were not interested so much in operating profits as in the quick returns to be had from stock manipulation.

But out of these manipulations, with the pyramiding of the value of the operating company's stock, came high electric rates for the consumer. It was shown in one study that ten utility companies valued in 1920 at $150,000,000 were in 1925 declared to be worth four times that amount. This increase in value was due not to assets acquired but rather to stock speculation on anticipated earnings of the companies. To pay dividends on the inflated stock, rates had to be kept high. In order to maximize the returns the utilities stayed in areas where there was the highest concentration of consumers.

In order to do all this the holding companies, and the operating executives who took their orders from the financial bosses, had to circumvent regulation by the states. This proved to be not too difficult. Jurisdiction of the state utility commissions supposed to carry out regulations and rate fixing was confined to the respective borders of each state. In contrast some holding companies operated in as many as thirty-three states. Both commissioners and technicians employed by most state-regulating commissions were woefully underpaid, and, for that matter, they still are. Holding companies could hire the most expensive legal and engineering talent in order to be sure to get what they wanted. Bribery and coercion were extended from the commissions to state legislatures.

The stock-market crash of 1929 underlined the top-heavy, senseless structure that had been put together by the big operators. No less than 128 companies were forced into bankruptcy or receivership. By 1938 arrears on holding company stock had reached many hundreds of millions of dollars, though net operating revenues stayed almost constant. The sensational stock-market investigation of 1930 disclosed many of the fantastic details of the piracy—it was scarcely less than that—that had brought on the debacle. And there were other investigations which exposed further dubious episodes in the long and sordid narrative.

Many knowledgeable observers had been insisting for years that regulation was futile or worse. Among them were the staunch advocates of public power. Year in and year out they had argued that since electric power was a monopoly and since the state regulation of the utilities was so patently a failure, the public development of power generation and distribution was obviously necessary if only as a means of trying to establish the costs of power production and distribution. These were for the most part men from the Midwest and the West. They represented rural areas where the feeling had grown through the years that eastern interests were conspiring against any justice for the farmer. They were in most instances Republicans, men like La Follette of Wisconsin, Borah of Idaho, McNary of Oregon, Brookhart of Iowa.

Outstanding among these men was George Norris of Nebraska. All through the twenties Norris had fought to keep the great power site of Muscle Shoals on the Tennessee River from being transferred to private ownership. It was largely due to his persistence, his tirelessness, his parliamentary skill that the whole area was saved for a broad and comprehensive development rather than being turned over to private interests that would have developed it in a restricted fashion. Time and again Norris stood up on the floor of the Senate to thwart the schemes of those who wanted to surrender the site for a mere fraction of its potential value.

The drive of Norris and the others for public power was one of the forces that helped to make rural electrification possible. Norris prepared the way for Tennessee Valley Authority and the other public power developments that have transformed the South and the Northwest. It is hardly conceivable that there could have been a major reduction in rates if it had not been for such developments. Therefore in a very real sense they made it possible to extend power on a large scale to America's farm homes at a cost that the farmer could pay.

To list all the individuals who helped prepare the political approach for expansion of the power industry, with Government playing a definite and important part, would be difficult or impossible. Among them were men like Benjamin Marsh, waging, with his People's Lobby in Washington, a constant battle for public ownership. These men knew little of the socialism of Europe and Karl Marx and they cared less about it. Public ownership in a monopoly industry like power had its roots in an American tradition growing directly out of the pioneering experience of the settlers who conquered the wilderness. Community barn raising, the common responsibility for road building and maintenance, the common ownership and exchange of such large pieces of machinery as threshing machines and combines—all illustrated this tradition. That kind of sharing was close to the experience of Norris, La Follette, and McNary. The transition from this to the public power dam was not too great. In the irrigation districts of the Far West was a pattern ready at hand.

The emotional and political force coming out of the years of discontent was now at full tide. In the chaotic and demoralized state in which it found itself, the private power industry was ill-equipped to resist the intrusion of public competition. But still another element was essential. That was the technical knowledge and competence to be able to initiate a workable system to bring electricity to American farms.

For many years Morris Llewellyn Cooke had studied the cost of power distribution. He had realized early that this was the key to over-all power costs, and a key carefully concealed in the mazes of utility cost accounting. Cooke made a unique contribution to rural electrification.

Of a well-to-do Pennsylvania family, he looked as unlike the picture of the radical New Dealer as it was possible to look. His father was a Quaker physician who was read out of the meeting for marrying the daughter of an Episcopalian minister. Cooke above all was a practical engineer with a great social conscience. He believed that there was always a practical way to get done what needed to be done.

While attending an eastern engineering school, Cooke spent his summers working as a newspaper reporter, first on the Denver *News* and later on New York and Philadelphia newspapers. His newspaper experience, while a brief interlude in his busy life, added much to the readability of his technical reports in later years.

Active in reform politics, Cooke became Director of Public Works in Philadelphia in 1915. Here Morris Cooke learned much about electric power companies and their rate structures. While in this position he won large rebates for the city of Philadelphia from a local utility company. At the same time he was studying the world-wide scope of the utility monopolies—gas, water, electric, and others. He lectured before college audiences on how electric rates were arrived at from outrageously watered stock issues, and the way in which utilities received rebates from their contractors.

In 1925 he worked as Director of the Giant Power Survey under Governor Gifford Pinchot of Pennsylvania. Pinchot, in describing the Giant Power Survey, foresaw the use of electricity on the farm. He wrote: "From the power field perhaps more than from any other quarter we can expect in the near future the most substantial aid in raising the standards of living, in eliminating the physical drudgery of life, and in winning the age-old struggle against poverty . . . . Our first concern must be with the small user . . . particularly the farmer. . . ." Working with Pinchot, the father of the conservation movement and one of the early advocates of rural electrification, Cooke broadened his social horizons. Many of the men who worked with him on the Giant Power Survey—Willard Herring, Harold Evans, Perry Taylor—later helped draw up the initial plans for a national rural electrification program. When Pinchot's power survey was completed, Cooke was recommended to Governor Franklin D. Roosevelt's staff as an adviser on public power in New York. Here in conjunction with other engineers, he continued to study the cost of distributing electricity to small farms.

Cooke's most important contribution to the start of the rural electrification program was this analysis of the cost of distributing power. This field—what might be called the retail area—had been suspect as the cover for high electric rates. The companies had long since determined exactly the costs of generating and transmitting electricity as far as the substation, and the facts about these wholesale costs had been widely published. The area between the substation and the customer's meter was unknown territory. It was believed to account for about half the cost of electricity to the domestic consumer.

Along with many other engineers, Cooke knew that rapid strides in perfecting generating and transmission equipment had made possible much cheaper electricity. He also knew that the demand for electricity had greatly increased since the days when it was used solely for lighting. The rapid expansion and development of ways to put the electric giant to work in industry and in the home should have changed the basis formerly used for computing rates. In the 1890s when electricity was used mostly between four and eight o'clock in the evening, the utility companies had to recover their costs during that brief period. This naturally meant higher electric rates. By 1925 the demand for electricity had become more or less constant throughout the day. As a consequence, the cost of operation could be recovered over a twenty-four hour period instead of necessarily being confined to a few hours.

Determined to crack the secret of distribution costs, Cooke and a staff of assistants itemized the expense of all the elements that went into the building of a power line—poles, transformers, wire, labor. He estimated the cost of engineers, of management, and of the overhead charges. Making a generous allowance for error, he still came up with the construction costs of power lines three to fifteen hundred dollars cheaper per mile than that given by the private power companies. In 1933 Cooke's figures were amplified before a meeting of engineers in New York by an electrical engineer named Clayton Pike. Pike was convinced that Cooke had finally solved the riddle of distribution costs.

The importance of the study that Cooke initiated can scarcely be stressed too much. By stripping away the mask of high distribution costs, he proved that it would be possible for the power companies to bring their lines out into the country for a fraction of the charge that had been considered standard up to then. Cooke realized, of course, that if the power companies were to build up their business and at the same time fulfill the social responsibility of giving service to everyone who wished it, they must of necessity cover whole areas with their lines and not follow certain favorable routes. Power Companies ran their power lines from town to town (and in many places still do today), picking up what business there was along the route of the line. Occasionally they went off the main road to hook up a very large user of electricity, such as a quarry or a sawmill.

But they ignored the smaller farms. Pointing to the experience of Sweden and other countries that had been successful in rural electrification, Cooke, as early as 1925, was urging upon the utility companies the policy of area coverage. He argued widely, with a great fund of technical knowledge, the necessity for spreading electricity far beyond the easy confines of town and city. Here was a major element in the whole complex of events that combined to bring about a revolution in rural America.

The catalyst was that master politician, Franklin Roosevelt. As with almost everything else that he did, Roosevelt personalized the forces that had brought rural electrification to a point at which a beginning could be made. On a scorching hot day in August of 1938, Roosevelt spoke to a crowd of forty thousand people at Barnesville, Georgia, who had come to hear him dedicate a co-operative utility financed by the the the Rural Electrification Administration. In the field around the speakers' platform were iceboxes, stoves, washing machines, and other bright, shiny new electrical equipment, proof of what power—electric power—meant to these Georgia farm people. In characteristic fashion, Roosevelt said:

"Fourteen years ago a Democratic Yankee came to a neighboring county in your state in search of a pool of warm water wherein he might swim his way back to health. . . . There was only one discordant note in that first stay of mine at Warm Springs. When the first-of-the-month bill came in for electric light for my little cottage, I found that the charge was eighteen cents a kilowatt hour—about four times what I pay at Hyde Park, New York. That started my long study of public utility charges for electric current and the whole subject of getting electricity into farm homes. . . . So it can be said that a little cottage at Warm Springs, Georgia, was the birthplace of the Rural Electrification Administration."

Almost as soon as he had become governor, Roosevelt plunged into the middle of an argument that has raged for nearly half a century. On the northern and western boundaries of the state formed by the St. Lawrence and Niagara rivers, New York has two of the largest potential hydroelectric resources in the nation—the St. Lawrence Rapids and Niagara Falls. The issue of whether private enterprise or the state should develop these two water-power sites had forced each governor through the years to be keenly aware of the nature of the public controversy. Governor Roosevelt believed strongly that electric power had become one of the necessities and not luxuries of modern life. He had seen in Warm Springs, when he went there in 1924 to build a run-down resort into an important medical foundation, that the high cost of electric power kept many people from benefiting from its use.

As governor, in his fight to permit the state of New York to develop the St. Lawrence Rapids, Roosevelt worked out the yardstick theory of public power development. He understood that regulation by state commissions was a failure, and he had come to think that perhaps a birch rod in the cupboard in the form of a state-owned and -operated electric system was essential to discipline the private power companies.

Thus he was prepared from the moment of his inauguration as President in 1933 to work with George Norris and the others who had for so long planned and dreamed of power projects that would bring down rates and carry this new magic of the twentieth century into every rural household. So the pieces fell into place one by one, and the reality of great power dams and thousands upon thousands of miles of line running into almost every county in America was now clearly foreshadowed.

Several years later, in 1936, Morris Cooke, then head of the Government's rural electrification program, attended a luncheon in New York arranged by the Electric Bond and Share Company to discuss the distribution of power in rural America. He recalls that in the course of the luncheon an elderly gentleman, clearing his throat ostentatiously, arose and asked Mr. Cooke if he had heard of the Red Wing, Minnesota, experiment. Yes, he replied, he knew all about it. By then, so fast was the new development coming on, it seemed as though he had been asked about an event in ancient history.

Chapter Three
WHO CAN DO THE JOB?

THE fundamental goal of the New Deal, for all its eccentricities and variations, was to get purchasing power into the pockets of those who were cut off from participation in the economy of the country. Greatly oversimplified for the purposes of politics, it was in essence the theory of compensatory spending by government as originated by John Maynard Keynes. In May of 1935 the popular phrase was "pump priming." President Roosevelt had just returned from a fishing trip to the Caribbean. A fund of five billion dollars had to be spent as quickly as the Roosevelt brain trust could devise ways of spending it; or, if that were possible, more quickly.

From this distance the atmosphere of that time seems more than a little incredible. Congress was on a spending spree, indignant at the President for his announced intention of vetoing the veterans' bonus bill which was then in process of passage with the active support of all veterans' groups. From the states came angry complaints that Washington was not getting the relief money out into the country quickly enough. The men around Roosevelt—Hopkins, Tugwell, Ickes—were besieging the White House for the requisite executive orders. On May 11, 1935, the President signed Executive Order 7037. That order established the Rural Electrification Administration.

Some time before, Roosevelt had persuaded Morris Cooke to postpone a vacation trip to Europe in order to head the contemplated new agency. Later in May Cooke and the nucleus of a staff moved into a big red brick Victorian house near Dupont Circle. It was a fitting commentary on the changing times that the house should have been lived in as one of Washington's show places by the late George Westinghouse who had contributed so much through invention and promotion to the electrical industry. This was the setting for the beginning agency that had only the broad instruction from the White House to "initiate a program to generate, transmit, and to distribute electricity in rural areas." That was a large order. How to carry it out was up to Cooke and the little group that started out with him.

In the White House planning stage rural electrification had been considered part of the national work relief program. One of the first to urge REA on the President as a relief objective was Ed O'Neal, then head of the American Farm Bureau Federation. The REA program tied into one bundle several of the New Deal's fondest hopes—low-cost power, conservation of natural resources, and the raising of the level of farm life.

Morris Cooke, with the backing of Harold Ickes, had presented in early 1934 the first complete plan for rural electrification. The plan covered the cost of carrying electricity to three and one half million farms. In this report, also, a Philadelphia lawyer, Vincent Nicholson, advised that the legality of such a rural electrification program would depend upon the welfare clause of the Constitution. Cooke found, as did others in later years, that without the participation of the federal Government, only a negligible part of rural electrification could be accomplished. As Morris Cooke wrote, ". . . perhaps the bizarre black-and-white-striped cover of this booklet kept it circulating amongst those in high places and so out of the wastebasket. . ." Whatever it might have been, this report helped insure that the federal government would make rural electrification an essential feature of the 1935 relief program.

Already, as a pioneer undertaking, the Alcorn County Electric Power Association had been organized to operate in and around the farm town of Corinth, Mississippi. Cheap power from Wilson Dam at Muscle Shoals enabled this nonprofit, civic-improvement corporation to cut electric rates in half during the first year of operation. Loans from TVA made it possible for the Alcorn Association to extend a hundred miles of rural lines. And the rates paid on those rural extensions were no more than those charged the townspeople of Corinth. After a year of operation the Alcorn co-operative had reduced its debt to TVA by one half. Here was an example to give hope to the new federal agency that had such a big job ahead of it and so few signposts to follow.

A stimulus of another kind came from the Mississippi Valley Report. In this report a group of specialists working under the direction of Cooke declared that only through active federal leadership and guidance "is any considerable electrification of dirt farms possible." This report was submitted to Secretary of the Interior Harold Ickes. It said that since farmers could afford radios, telephones, and automobiles, then certainly they could pay for electricity at reasonable rates. The real difficulty was not the farmers' inability to pay, the report found, but the indifference was evidenced by high line costs, high power costs, and almost universal restrictions covering line extensions.

Originally the electrification program, as written into the Emergency Relief Act of 1935, was to have been administered by Harry Hopkins. His chief engineer, blunt, bluff, hard-driving John Carmody, had been considering plans for the program. Carmody had found some guidance, which was to stand him in good stead when he later became deputy administrator of REA, in what North Carolina had accomplished during the previous three years.

North Carolina's progressive Governor J. C. Blucher Ehringhaus had made rural electrification a major issue in his 1932 campaign after a North Carolina state college survey had shown that only one farm in a hundred in his state had central station electricity. The strong farm support he received as a result of this stand encouraged Ehringhaus to press his plan to electrify his state. Extensive surveys were made. As a result of these surveys in 1934 the North Carolina legislature created a state electrification authority. Later in the same year a bill was passed permitting the formation of nonprofit companies to carry out the distribution of power to the farms.

Fairly early in the planning stage it had become obvious to Hopkins and Carmody that the program was too technical for inclusion in a relief agency. Cooke, the new administrator, soon discovered that the specifications for relief spending were incompatible with an engineering development. First of all, it was not possible to use large amounts of unskilled labor in planning and building rural power lines. Secondly, the need to spend money quickly precluded any careful planning such as was necessary for a program of this type.

The first exploratory beginning was hesitant and slow. During this first summer Roosevelt asked Cooke if he was following the directives the President had issued covering all relief projects. The answer, of course, was "No." And so the President, in his genial, offhand way, said, "Well, Morris, then I'll have to cut you off the pay roll."

Finding the REA could not operate as the established relief agencies did, the President modified the directive under which Administrator Cooke was trying to start the REA program. In August the President transformed REA into a loan agency. After a legal tiff with the Comptroller General's office, the agency began to plan its projects on a self-liquidating basis. The latter decision was, in the opinion of H. S. Pearson, consulting economist for REA, probably the most far-reaching fundamental policy decision in the history of the agency.

The necessity for using relief labor on technical projects requiring engineers, linemen, and other experts was now removed. Even more important, the electrification program would not be one of grant and subsidy. It would be self-supporting. So at last REA was ready to begin an orderly program of lending on a self-liquidating basis.

But this was still not the end of the exploratory period. The problem of how to get electricity to the farms in the shortest possible time remained. There were three ways to do the job under a loan program—through private companies, through municipalities with publicly owned plants, or through nonprofit co-operatives. Since the urgency was always to prime the pump with money eagerly appropriated by Congress, it was important to begin the building of rural lines immediately, and obviously there could be no prolonged debate over method.

Because the private companies, with their construction crews, their engineers, and territory franchises, seemed to be in a position to undertake the program at once, Cooke turned first to them. Several months before the agency was finally created, Cooke and several of his associates had been in consultation with the representatives of private utilities to determine how they could take a part in an REA program. Nine days after the President issued his order, fifteen of the largest companies sent representatives to a formal conference in the Department of the Interior Building. On that occasion the executives were amiable and apparently receptive, but they were also noncommittal. The only result of that meeting was an agreement by the utility men to appoint a committee to survey "the extent to which further development of rural electrification may be promptly effected in co-operation with the Rural Electrification Administration." Two months later the committee submitted its report to Administrator Cooke.

The utility companies presented a program calling for the investment of over a quarter of a billion dollars during the first year. But there was a big catch in this proposal. Private companies knew that they would have to lower farm rates and simplify their rate schedules before they could obtain REA loans. Either they found it impossible to do this or they were unwilling.

Their report said, "to immediately attempt to standardize rate schedules nationally would necessitate the revision of rates for three million consumers under numerous jurisdictions . . . The difficulties that would rise would be such that the program would be delayed indefinitely." The report by the private companies added that ". . . the problem of the farmer is not one of rates, but of financing the wiring and purchase of appliances." How much the private companies were in error in understanding the problem of the farmer can be shown by the fact that today just one per cent of REA loans have gone to help the farmer wire his premises, install water systems, and purchase appliances. The farmer has proved himself quite able to afford appliances, and in fact has spent nearly four times the amount he has borrowed from REA installing various electrical machines on his farm. The utility companies further showed their misunderstanding of rural electrification by the statement: "Rural customers are the most favored class of customers to which service is rendered . . ." This was remarkable in view of the fact that at that time less than ten per cent of American farmers had electric power.

The report ended by saying that the urge for rural electrification was a social rather than an economic problem. If the industry was to undertake the job, then government would have to make the companies long-term, low-interest loans. Considering the whole field of rural electrification in the United States, the companies believed that there were "very few farms requiring electricity for major farm operations that are not already served."

But behind these smooth-sounding words which farm leaders found so incomprehensible in view of the demand they knew to exist at the grass roots, there may have been other and more compelling reasons for, in effect, a refusal to work with REA. The utility industry was locked in mortal combat with the Roosevelt Administration over the proposed holding company bill. All the considerable force of the utilities had been marshaled to block the passage of that bill, which was intended to divorce operating electric companies from the grip of the financing companies that had scooped them up like so many fish in giant nets.

The suspicion was widely reported that the electric industry was waging what amounted to a capital equipment strike against the Administration as one weapon in the struggle. Therefore, the companies were not interested in a big program of capital investment such as REA proposed.

The conflict over the holding company bill, sponsored by Senator Burton K. Wheeler of Montana and Representative Sam Rayburn of Texas, was one of the bitterest in the whole history of the New Deal. A leading warrior was Wendell Willkie, then chairman of the board of the holding company known as Commonwealth and Southern.

The shock-headed, quick-talking Willkie told a meeting of utility executives in New York about the effort to compromise the provision in the Wheeler-Rayburn Bill providing the death sentence for holding companies. Under the compromise, according to Willkie, the industry proposed that the Government should halt its program to generate and transmit power. It would build no further hydroelectric projects. In return, the electric industry would submit to "impartial regulation." The companies would increase their funds for expansion and spend "substantial amounts of money in rural areas." Roosevelt's refusal to consider this compromise, said Willkie, had kept over three billion dollars from being spent for consumer and producer goods. In an effort to make the Government back down, the industry had spent more than five million dollars. But the effort had failed. And then Willkie said with vehemence that was later to make him such a fiery stump speaker:

"Utility properties cannot be expanded, rates cannot be reduced; capital expenditures cannot be made against the calamities of the threatened invasion of a business by the Government."

But whether the reason was that there were so "few farms not served," as the committee of utility executives had reported, or whether Wendell Willkie had expressed it more frankly when he declared that the industry could not make investments in the face of the Government's attitude, the fact remains that the private companies faded out of the REA picture. Of the first ten projects authorized by November 1935, only one was that of a private utility.

By March 1936, of the twenty-seven loans authorized, five went to private utilities.

Even before the private utilities, or most of them, had shown that they were unwilling or unable to co-operate in the rural electrification program, Cooke had begun to approach the other groups. He announced at this time that he "desired the best minds in the country in planning this program, so I have been consulting municipalities, private companies, and co-operatives." Municipalities seemed to offer great promise in carrying power lines to the farms. Many cities such as Los Angeles had been furnishing farmers and fruit growers electricity for years at a city rate.

In November of 1935 a conference of municipal managers was held at Kansas City. There was criticism of the municipalities for being slow to grasp the idea of extending their lines into rural territory. But serious obstacles to such a development were pointed out by others at the conference.

In 1935 the Missouri Supreme Court had ruled that municipalities could not carry their lines beyond the corporate limits of the city. The court held that the farmer could come to the boundary of a city and tap power from a municipal plant, but the municipality could not take a line to the farmer. While the Missouri court had pointed out that this was not necessarily a permanent prohibition, to extend municipal lines beyond the radius agreed upon by charter would certainly be to get involved illegally with the private utilities. In addition to that, townspeople were fearful that to extend the lines from the city to the country would mean higher rates for them. This attitute may have come partly out of the constant propaganda of the private companies. For towns that paid most of their taxes out of the earnings of publicly owned electric power plants, it was not good politics to talk about rural extensions with low returns or no returns at all.

During this uncertain experimental period, letters were pouring into Washington from farmers all over the country. They had heard about REA and they wondered what the reason was for the delay. A rancher in Colorado wrote that he had read "where a man had been appointed to have charge of a committee or bureau where the President wished to have farms electrified." Where could he find out about it, the rancher wanted to know. A farmer in Indiana wrote to the President to say that he and all his neighbors were interested in getting power for their farms. He had become so anxious for electricity that the other morning he had mounted his "good, black saddle-horse" and had ridden around his neighbors' farms. He and his neighbors were anxious to help themselves, the letter said, and as proof of their sincerity they were sending the President a petition with forty-six names signed to it, asking his help in getting power lines. Cooke advised these farmers how to go about getting electricity:

"Find out how many farmers living within, say five or ten miles of your home in any direction would pay for electricity if they could get it at a moderate price. Ask them about how much they would use—and for what purpose—grinding feed, heating water, preserving fruit in an electric refrigerator and, of course, lighting their houses and pumping water. When you have the facts, send them in to us."

As farmers began to furnish this information, it became apparent that rural electrification was to take a middle way. Co-operatives were coming to the front as the principal borrowers. Seven of the first ten loans were made to co-operative organizations. A co-operative in Boone County, Indiana, one in Miami County, Ohio, another in the Bartlett community of Texas, and in Monroe County, Mississippi, received the first REA loans announced in November of 1935. Other loans were made at the same time to public power districts in Nebraska, to the state of South Carolina, and to the city of Dayton, Tennessee. Only one loan was made to a private utility company; the Central Iowa Power Company received six thousand dollars to build three miles of line. By the end of 1936 nearly one hundred co-operatives in twenty-six states had signed loan contracts with REA.

"It became apparent," Morris Cooke wrote in his first annual report, "that the [private] industry was not even going to use a portion of the funds available for rural electrification, and farm organizations of a co-operative character forged to the front as the principal borrowers under the REA program."

But there was considerable uncertainty and no little conflict before this development could really get going in a large way. The co-operative idea was a familiar one in most farm areas and particularly where Scandinavians, Finns, and Germans had settled. They knew what co-operatives had meant in the "old country."

For native-born Americans, there was nothing alien about the concept either. The co-operative idea had been linked to political protest movements such as that of the Populists. The co-operative approach spread rapidly, and by the turn of the century co-operative grain elevators were located throughout the Midwest and particularly in Minnesota and the Northwest. In 1914 the first electric co-operative was formed in this country. By 1935 there were at least thirty such co-operatives providing electricity to farmers.

The latter were all small developments. The largest of them had just sixty-three miles of line and 350 members. A small co-operative lacked the kind of engineering, legal advice, and financial resources available to private utilities. Yet despite these handicaps a majority of them had somehow managed to survive. But the inherent limitations of the early electric co-operatives made the idea seem risky to

Cooke and some of the other engineers he brought into REA.

On the other hand, the success of the Alcorn Co-operative in the TVA area seemed to be proof that such an organization was capable of extending electric power to the farms. And in the end it appeared that there was no other way to do the job that farmers were with ever increasing insistence demanding that the Administration get on with.

Serious doubts were expressed within the co-operative movement itself that rural electrification with government loans was a proper function. One of the dedicated leaders of the movement in America was James Warbasse, long head of the Co-operative League of the U.S.A. Absorbed in the ideology of co-operation and somewhat removed from its practical aspects, Warbasse's view was that of the theorist who feels that any variation from the orthodox concept is bound to be harmful. He felt strongly that the state and the co-operative movement had interests so opposed as to make any harmonious relationship impossible. One exists for the commonwealth, the other for private individuals banded together.

"Should the co-operative movement," Warbasse wrote, "combine with the political state, the natural outcome would be the state would take co-operation under its control. This would be a calamity to an independent self-help enterprise." In 1935 Warbasse and others in the movement were urging Cooke not to use the co-operative system to promote rural electrification. But events had already forced the administrator's hand.

Senator Norris was disappointed at the end of 1935 with the progress of REA, as was Cooke himself. They both saw the need for a more positive, long-range program outside the restrictive framework of a mere relief project. Accordingly, they began an exchange of letters such as frequently pass between legislator and administrator preparatory to the drafting of a bill. Senator Norris believed that a "concrete plan for area coverage should be stressed so that all farms would get electric power." He was also strongly of the opinion that the law should specifically exclude private companies from the federal rural electrification program. The news that George Norris, father of the TVA, was preparing a new rural electrification program to be included in a bill to be introduced in the House by Representative Rayburn of Texas caused widespread political repercussions.

At their annual convention in California the National Grange supported Norris's idea of a permanent REA program. They felt as he did, that it should be carried out by public agencies or by co-operatives. The Grange resolved that private companies be forbidden the use of public funds to build lines or electric substations. Similarly, the conservative American Farm Bureau Federation, meeting a month later in Chicago, urged farmers to form co-operatives so they might obtain electricity at the lowest possible cost. This powerful support from two of America's most politically influential and conservative farm organizations did much to hasten the appearance of the Norris-Rayburn Bill in early 1936.

By this time, however, the private utilities had been aroused from their lethargy. Abruptly they abandoned the position that neither they nor the farmers could afford to bring power to the farm. During 1935 the number of farms newly electrified by private companies increased 175 per cent. And the private utilities promised that during the following year the increase would be even greater. In 1935 they spent over five times what REA did.

While the private companies' rural line building was greater in volume than REA's in the first years, they did rural electrification considerable harm. For the companies extended their lines only to selected areas and ignored the principle of area coverage. This practice cut the heart out of many proposed co-operative districts and prevented some farms from receiving electricity for many years. Farmers denounced these spur lines of the electric companies as "spite lines."

They were convinced that such spite lines were being built in undeveloped territory to skim the cream off what would otherwise have been co-operative districts and to protect the utility franchises that might otherwise have been pre-empted. There were, of course, notable exceptions, such as the Georgia Power Company, which from the beginning of REA advertised its willingness to assist co-operatives and renounced any intentions of "skimming off the cream." But where spite lines were built, they produced hatred and resentment that were long to plague the private utilities.

While all the companies rushed construction crews into the field, utility executives were waging war on the Washington front. In hearings before Congress on the Norris-Rayburn Bill, they uttered dire warnings to the effect that nonprofit agencies could not possibly carry on the distribution of electric power over a wide area and were therefore bound to fail. The co-operatives were without experience, existing assets, assured income. How could they hope to succeed? The private utilities also complained that it was discriminatory for Congress to exclude them from the REA program. They were best equipped to rush the program to completion and they had drawn up plans to do so. As many farm leaders noted, this attitude was in marked contrast to that of a year before when they had seen hardly any reason for the effort at all.

The fiercest debate in Congress centered on this question as to whether private companies should be allowed to borrow from REA. In the House the opposition to the utilities came for the most part from representatives from the West, the South, and the Southwest. In the Pacific states the fight between public and private power had long been bitter. It had served to precipitate into national prominence such men as the late Senator Hiram Johnson. Representatives from the South and Southwest smarted under a deep sense of injustice. They came from communities where the soil was eroded through long overwork under a cash-crop system. As they had come to see it, their resources were constantly being drained off, and resources in men as well as in materials, to enrich a little area on the eastern seaboard of the United States.

Foremost among these representatives with a fiery sense of ancient grievance was John Rankin of Mississippi. Rankin came from an impoverished area that was being transformed by the low-cost power of TVA. To many he was the prototype of the southern demagogue, demanding that the authority of the federal Government be used to redress the balance between the rich and arrogant North and the long-neglected South. He was of that generation of southern dissidents who were filled with resentment at the injustice of discriminatory freight rates which helped to keep the South in the status of a colonial hewer of wood and drawer of water.

But whatever anyone might think of him, there was no denying Rankin's force. He stood on the floor of the House and shouted, "If you begin lending to private corporations, they will do with it just what they are doing with their money now, and that is building a few scattered lines out in the rural sections, paralyzing and preventing real rural electrification." Rankin demanded that a provision granting loans to "persons or corporations" be struck out of the Norris-Rayburn Bill. A congressman from Connecticut replying, said that rural electrification would "go on faster if Congress and the Administration would remove from the companies the fear of being murdered."

Both in committee and on the floor of the House, a heated argument went on over whether the United States was in fact woefully behind the rest of the world in rural electrification. Spokesmen for the utility industry had in committee hearings called this claim made for foreign countries "irrelevant and entirely misleading." They argued that if factors of geography and density of population were considered, the United States would be found to be far in advance of other countries. Connecticut's Representative Schuyler Merritt repeated this statement on the floor. Knowing that the farming area from Montana to the Atlantic seaboard was less than ten per cent electrified, Rankin rose in wrath to make Merritt swallow his words. The exchange between them was as follows:

Rankin: The gentleman says electric service is quite new. Of course it is no more new in this country than in Europe.

Merritt: If you compare [Europe] with the eastern states or California I think the results are as satisfactory here as they are there.

Rankin: I wonder if the gentleman knows that in New Zealand two-thirds of their farms are electrified, [and] in the United States about ten per cent are. . . .

Merritt: In New Zealand they deal with enormous tracts of land . . . . Also New Zealand is a socialistic state. . . .

Rankin: I wonder if the gentleman knows that in France and Germany ninety per cent of their farms are electrified. Those are not socialistic states.

Merritt: No, they are not socialistic, but they are imperialistic.

Rankin: I wonder if the gentleman knows that Holland and Switzerland are practically 100 per cent electrified?

Merritt: But they are no larger than our New England.

Rankin: I understand that there is no state in New England that has even twenty-five per cent of its rural farms electrified.

Merritt: I do not care to give the gentleman more time.

The dispute over permitting participation by private power companies was finally resolved by Sam Rayburn, whose rare speeches have always carried weight in the House. Rayburn argued "that there are so many rural communities in the country that cannot qualify, that cannot possibly convince any sane director of rural electrification that they have enough to bring into existence a co-operative or corporation that can live, much less even make itself a self-liquidating proposition" that the private utilities should not be excluded from the program.

While Rankin and his followers were defeated on this issue, they clung to their hard-bitten belief in the promise of public power. They hoped that the federally financed REA program might advance the goal of public power, and were somewhat disappointed in the middle approach the program took. These men, extremists, fanatical even in the view of some, provided the drive and vitality to put over the rural electric power program. Called the "roughnecks" by Morris Cooke, they fought for REA's large appropriations in Congress. They kept watchful guard over the program, preventing it from being killed in the obscurity of committee rooms. These roughnecks saw that hopes and plans were translated into action.

The REA Act of 1936 provided for several types of loans. The first type was to be used for building electric power lines and for generating and transmitting electricity. Another type of loan was to enable the farmer to buy electrical equipment. Under the first heading preference was to be given to borrowers other than private companies. These loans were to be self-liquidating within twenty-five years, and the borrower was to pay the same rate of interest that the Government paid on its long-term obligations.

Loans for electrical equipment were to cover wiring the farm house, installing a water system, or buying ranges, refrigerators, washing machines, or electric irons. As in the act creating TVA passed three years earlier, the Norris-Rayburn Bill specified that politics was to be kept out of REA. It was specified that "this act shall be administered entirely on a nonpartisan basis, and in the appointment of officials and the selection of employees . . . no political test or qualifications shall be permitted or given consideration." Should the administrator violate this section, the bill provided that the President remove him from office. With Roosevelt's signature on May 20, 1936, the REA as we know it today came into being. The act determined the pattern that the development of power on the farm was henceforward to take. The co-operative was to do the job that private industry had failed to do.

But Senator Norris's insistence that the program be self-liquidating made it necessary for REA to solve many problems confronting eager co-operators waiting on the doorstep of the agency. It was necessary to devise legal, economic, and engineering tests in order to appraise the ability of a proposed co-operative to become a financially sound business. Legal codes varying from state to state determine the form that the co-ops can take. The structure of the co-operatives had to be such that the members would not lose control of their company to those who might want to destroy it. Engineers had to design lines that were cheap yet durable. In order to obtain wholesale power, negotiations had to be undertaken with utilities that were often antagonistic. REA investigators had to determine whether or not there was a sufficient number of farm homes within the area to justify making a loan. A capable manager had to be found for each co-operative, one who would be both engineer and administrator.

From the first, Cooke realized that such a complex and difficult program could be carried out under the direction only of those sympathetic with the concept. He interviewed personally each applicant for a position in the agency to determine whether he was in sympathy with the goals of REA. The staff he built up was one of the major contributions of his administration, and it was in no small measure responsible for the remarkably sound structure of the rural electrification program.

His deputy, Carmody, a successful industrial engineer and experienced executive, was working equally hard trying to standardize details of the co-operative system of power lines. He organized a development section that, contrary to the usual relationship between lender and borrower, helped co-operatives draw up their plans that were to be presented to REA as a basis for their loan applications. In February of 1937, when the energetic Carmody took Cooke's place as administrator, the foundation of the program had been laid. Ninety-four projects costing more than twenty million dollars were under construction or completed. On nearly thirty projects power was already being transmitted. As Cooke himself had foreseen when he had agreed to take the post of administrator for a short period the phase of the architect was at an end. It was now the turn of the hard driver bent on getting results.

Yet there were many, believing apparently that rural America could be lighted up overnight, who were impatient with what had been done up to that time. Paul Ward of the Baltimore *Sun*, writing in *The Nation*, said that "REA stands today as one of F.D.R.'s worst failures." Reflecting a fairly wide section of opinion in the New Deal, he charged that both the municipally owned plants and the co-operatives had been thwarted until the utilities could kill them through spite lines. According to Ward, Cooke and others in the REA believed, "God never intended to electrify America unless the latter-day Insulls and Hopsons first assented."

Those who were close to the trials and errors of the experimental period could hardly have foreseen the extraordinarily swift development of the years just ahead. It is one of the most impressive stories in the history of American agriculture and industry. What has taken place is a peaceful revolution transforming farm life in America. All the preliminary spadework had been done and done thoroughly. This was a threshold, a beginning.

It had come out of a long-pent-up demand to raise standards on the farm somewhat closer to those prevailing in the cities. But always it was that insistence from out in the country which moved the program forward.

Chapter Four
THE UNCEASING STRUGGLE

SINCE 1932 the federal Government and the private power industry in this country have been engaged in almost continuous warfare. There have been occasional periods of temporary truce when the struggle seemed about to be resolved. In some areas, and under special circumstances, the two forces have achieved a mutually satisfactory relationship.

To anyone viewing it objectively, this warfare must seem a very curious phenomenon. Each year the twenty-billion-dollar private electric light and power industry expands both its operations and its profits. Part of the four billion dollars the industry earns in serving over one hundred million people goes into advertisements that speak in dire warning of the threat of nationalization. These advertisements talk about "federal socialism" eating away at the roots of American free enterprise.

It is true, of course, that the percentage of all the power produced in this country coming from federal hydroelectric projects is today roughly ten per cent, and virtually all of this has come into being during the past twenty years. It is also true that these publicly owned projects are of a magnitude that could have been undertaken only by Government with a concern for flood control, conservation, and the raising of marginal standards of living in certain regions. The Tennessee Valley Authority in the Southeast, Hoover Dam in the West, Grand Coulee and Bonneville in the Pacific Northwest are on a scale that could never have been achieved by private risk capital. It has been repeatedly argued that, therefore, these projects should never have been undertaken at all, since the appropriation of federal funds for this purpose was immoral and destructive of private enterprise.

But certain realities cannot be ignored. Without the power of the TVA it would never have been possible to have produced sufficient aluminum to make fifty thousand airplanes a year during World War II.

Nor would it have been possible to have operated the giant plant for nuclear fission at Hanford, Washington, without the great hydroelectric projects in the Pacific Northwest. Wartime industries could never have been established there nor would it have been possible to have given jobs in the postwar era to the greatly increased population of that rapidly growing part of America.

But however large the area of debate about federally built power plants, the continuing attack of the power industry on the rural electrification program carried out on a pay-as-you-go, loan basis must seem to have an element of irrationality in it. First, as has been shown, the REA at the outset made a genuine effort to persuade the power industry to build the essential lines with the assistance of loans such as were later approved to co-operatives. A prerequisite was that rates be lowered to farm consumers. The utilities said that this was impossible and found other good and sufficient reasons why they could not participate in the program, their final conviction being that in any event it was bound to fail. Yet today nearly three million co-operative members pay to the private power industry about $43,000,000 annually for about sixty per cent of the current they consume. This new business has grown out of the REA program initiated in 1935. While it is a comparatively small fraction of the total revenue of the industry, it is increasing by leaps and bounds, the increase for 1950 over 1949 being twenty per cent.

When they appeared before Congress to oppose the Norris-Rayburn Bill to create a permanent REA, spokesmen for the utilities took a scornful attitude. It was all a crackpot experiment and doomed to fail. The attitude was, "Let them build the lines. When they fail we can buy them out for ten cents on the dollar."

But when Senator Norris introduced his measure providing over four hundred million dollars for a ten-year electrification plan, the power companies sprang into action. They sent construction crews out into the country to pick off the best part of the rural market before the co-operatives could be formed and get their plans approved in Washington. For the industry this was a kind of insurance, since after all the government REA program might not fail so completely as they had anticipated.

In Harrison County, West Virginia, the president of the local utility had in 1936 told the county agent there that the company would build only three and a half miles of rural line. But the farmers of Harrison County organized an REA co-operative. The company was suddenly galvanized into action, building 150 miles of line through sections most readily served. That kind of service was contrary to the area coverage which the engineers of REA believed to be essential if all the farmers in a given district were to get electricity.

Prophesying failure for the REA experiment, the utilities had their ablest attorneys at work searching for ways and means to checkmate the co-operatives. One question still undecided was whether the co-operatives should come under the control of state utility commissions. Here was an advantageous point of attack. Farmers would band together to organize their co-operatives. They would send a loan application into Washington. Immediately the power company in the area would claim that the proposed co-operative was about to infringe upon its franchised territory. The company had been on the verge of planning the electrification of this particular rural district itself. Therefore, let the co-operative show the state utility commission if there was necessity for it to build in the area.

The whole concept of utility regulation by a public commission had been reviewed by both Roosevelt and Norris. Both men felt that the attempt to regulate a monopoly industry in the interest of a reasonable rate to the consumer at a reasonable profit for the company had failed. Case after case could be cited to show that regulatory commissions were either too weak or inexperienced or, worse, that they had come under the control of those interests that they were supposed to regulate. The reason for this situation was summed up very well in an opinion by the late federal Judge T. Alan Goldsborough:

"You see, any commission of this kind has a continual pressure on them. . . . The public utilities all have a force of experts. . . . They have a force of experts who are subtly bringing pressure all the time on the commission to take some action which will increase the income of the utilities; and not only are they doing it, but in a lesser degree, the experts of the commissions, and the commission's, and the people's counsel are doing the same thing.

"The reason is this. Not that they—the commissions' experts and the people's counsel—are corrupt, but that they do not expect to be connected with the commissions forever. And the only future lies in connecting themselves with a public utility; and therefore the natural trend of their minds is toward the public utilities. And that is the situation that the commissions are confronted with all the time."

In some states the utility commissions have been sympathetic and helpful in aiding the co-operatives to get started. But in general the leaders of the rural electrification movement have felt that it was best not to be under the control of a regulatory commission. They based their view on the legal premise that, unlike a private utility company, there is no public interest to protect when consumers band together for their own mutual good. In an electric power co-operative the distributor and owner on the one hand and the consumer on the other hand are one and the same person. Since they are the same, there is no need for the state to protect the individual consumer who is, in this instance, responsible for his own business, including the rates he pays. Eventually this point of view was accepted by three fourths of the states in which utility commissions have partially or wholly exempted co-operatives from their jurisdiction.

By 1938 it was obvious to the power companies that, in spite of all they had said to the contrary, the farm market had great potentialities. The inexperienced co-operatives that they had expected to fail were flourishing and rapidly expanding. The amount of electricity used by the farmer exceeded even what REA's engineers had estimated. Three hundred and fifty REA co-operatives were functioning and they showed constantly increasing revenues as more and more farmers signed up. Larger appropriations for REA loans were pushed through Congress by "the roughnecks," and as the program expanded the average cost of building an electric power line fell by half, to less than nine hundred dollars a mile. Here was a tangible development that the utilities could not brush aside with rhetoric. They began with far more energy to initiate a competitive building program.

A basic conflict developed that has left a heritage of bitterness. The private companies insisted that what they were doing was straightforward competition to get at least a part of the market that REA had revealed. But co-operative leaders and those in charge of the program in Washington were convinced that these were for the most part spite lines intended to cripple or destroy a co-operative when it was projected or after it was started. In instance after instance they could show how this belated competition from the private companies served to hamper or destroy the possibility of area coverage through a co-operative organization.

The pattern was fairly uniform. Here is a small co-operative in a moderately prosperous rural community. The plans for the project as submitted to Washington provide for about twenty-six miles of line to serve only about one hundred members. The local power company hears that the line is about to be approved. Promptly the company drives a seven-mile power line through the middle of the project. In this way it picks up thirty-five of the co-operative's best prospective customers. Without these thirty-five customers the project is not practicable. Consequently REA is forced to refuse the loan. Then the sixty-five other farm households come to the company with the request to be hooked up too. And the company replies that it is not profitable to serve any others than those already on the compact seven-mile line. Therefore, sixty-five households that might have had electricity are forced to go without.

In the prosperous corn belt a private utility had a 22,000-volt line running along a road connecting two towns. For years the company had declined to serve the farm households within easy reach of that line. The reason given was that the amount of electricity the farmers would use would not justify the cost of building a low-voltage line to serve them. After REA was established, these same farmers organized a co-operative to get electricity for themselves. When news of the formation of the co-operative got around, the company promptly built a low-voltage line, hooking up the larger and more prosperous farms along the highway. Without these larger users the REA loan could not be paid off and the co-operative had to be disbanded.

If this had happened in a few isolated instances, farm leaders would not have come to suspect that this was a deliberate strategy of the power companies. But more than two hundred co-ops in forty states were faced with the tactic of the spite line. Eight of these co-operatives were completely wiped out. Others suffered long and hampering delays. Still others were forced to overcome obstacles that would not have been in the way had it not been for this belated effort of the power industry to take that part of the market which had been so long ready and waiting for development.

There were variations in the pattern. In Georgia the Georgia Power Company co-operated fully and openly with REA co-operatives. In neighboring Alabama the Alabama Power Company fought a long and harassing war against the co-operatives both in the field through competition, and in the courts. At least seven Alabama co-ops were destroyed or crippled by power company lines that skimmed the cream off the business.

One such case involving the Cherokee County Electric Co-operative gained wide attention. Testifying in one of the court proceedings in the case, Farmer Williamson said that he had been trying to get the power company to build a line to his farm home for ten years. They had told him that the business would not be sufficient to justify construction of such a line. But when he and his neighbors applied to REA for a loan, the power company "jumped in and built the line without even asking us to sign up for it." At the same time the power company sent in agents who told the farmers that to become part of an electric co-operative would be equivalent to putting a mortgage on each farm home. These agents spread scare stories to the effect that each farm would be personally responsible for the full amount of the government loan. Farmers were told that co-op members would be liable for accidents occurring on the power lines. One farmer was told by a company agent, "Why, the power will be so weak out here that your light bulb will only glow red."

The Alabama Power Company insisted that the line it was building was in no sense a spite line. The company said the line was in territory covered by a company franchise, the construction was in the normal course of operation, it was in response to local demand. The company raised, too, an argument that has been heard again and again in the course of the long dispute over public versus private power. Company lines were built before those of the co-operative, so the argument went, and therefore the co-operative proposed to duplicate existing facilities.

The REA is forbidden by law to serve farmers already having power. Therefore the Alabama Company asked the court to cut off the flow of funds from the Administration in Washington to the Cherokee County Co-operative. Replying to the company's suit, Vincent Nicholson, REA attorney, said: "The company lines were not constructed for legitimate business reasons but for the purpose of interfering with the project organized by the Cherokee Co-operative." Nicholson told the court that the great majority of

Cherokee members had served notice on the company that they did not want its service and would not take it. The court dismissed the company's complaint and this was considered a signficant victory.

This bitter competition in building lines was suspended with the beginning of World War II in 1941. The reason was a shortage of construction materials which stopped most line building. Copper, aluminum, and steel were vital materials critically needed in war production. Electric energy became so scarce in many areas that it was necessary to impose a brown-out.

While new lines could not be built or energized except on a limited basis, it was clear that there would be a tremendous pent-up demand for electricity on farms that had not yet been brought into the program. Word of the transformation that electricity could work had spread far and wide. Young men leaving the farm to go into the armed services would not be content to come back to the older order of the kerosene lamp and the hand pump. For the farmers of America electricity was no longer a luxury. It was not just a convenience. It had become a necessity.

A leading farm magazine, *Country Gentleman*, made a survey in 1944 of the market that postwar rural electrification would provide. The magazine found that "there are many bright spots on the postwar market horizon but probably none holds forth more promise than rural electrification, which is mutually beneficial to both rural populations and private industry. By relieving many of the physical burdens that have been the heritage of rural America for generations and by increasing agricultural productivity and income, rural electrification can bring a higher standard of living. From the standpoint of productivity, it opens new markets and broadens old ones, thus contributing materially to employment and profits. . . ." The survey found that more that a billion dollars would be spent on appliances by farmers getting central station electricity. The rural plumbing market alone—water pumps, kitchen sinks, and bathtubs—was estimated at $350,000,000. It was a golden market, a bonanza, that beckoned private enterprise.

The power industry reduced its attempts to compete in the field with REA co-operatives. The aim now was to keep sole ownership over generating and transmission facilities that would supply this rapidly developing market. Another line of attack developed and that was to try to take over co-operatives wherever they showed signs of faltering. Of course, if the co-operative failed to maintain standards, if the members were apathetic or indifferent, if the management was poor, trouble and dissatisfaction were bound to follow.

In 1937 for the first time a power company bought out a co-operative. In Johnston County, North Carolina, the Carolina Power and Light Company paid $11,000 for a co-op project that was still on the drawing boards. Although the co-op had won a State Supreme Court decision against the power company in order to get permission to build its power lines, the company seems to have had little difficulty in persuading the directors to sell. The court, however, sharply criticized those who had authorized the transactions because they had not consulted the members of the co-operative. Nevertheless, the court ruled that they had the right to sell out.

In the postwar years a number of companies tried to buy out co-operative rivals. But Appalachian Power, Idaho Power, Pacific Gas and Electric, and the Consumers Power Company of Michigan found it a great deal more difficult than in the first instance. Rural electrification in 1937 was still a dubious experiment. By 1948 rural electrical co-operatives numbered nearly a thousand. Membership totalled nearly two million farm families. The co-ops were welded together by the National Rural Electric Co-operative Association, which kept careful watch over the progress and problems of member co-ops. In most instances the co-operatives were multimillion-dollar corporations with several thousand members intensely proud of the business they had built up. In many states co-operatives had set up statewide organizations to co-ordinate the interests of the member groups within the states.

Obviously against such strength the utilities could make little headway. But where they found weaknesses they were quick to exploit them. Some co-ops, for example, had power shortages. This meant low voltage on the lines, and this in turn resulted in discontented farm membership. Other co-ops had poor management and consequently members did not get service comparable to that which the private utility could furnish. Office records were snarled, applications for service had piled up. Members were angry at the careless way in which the co-op had cleared rights of way through valuable farming land. And there were frequent power outages on the lines.

In most instances where the utilties sought to buy out the co-op, the relationship between members and management was indifferent or poor. Farm members had signed up without having very much idea of what a co-operative enterprise meant or what it entailed in responsibility. This was an invitation to the utility to send in skillful public-relations men who could further confuse and divide an uncertain membership. At the same time, of course, the company wanted a good financial prospect in a prosperous farm area. The utilities preferred older co-ops that had built up their line load and that had wide area coverage. And a record of good bill collections was also important.

One co-op with the requisite defects and virtues was the Craig-Botetourt Electrical Co-operative with headquarters in the sleepy Virginia town of New Castle. The Craig-Botetourt was organized in

1937 to serve the upland farms in the wooded mountain region at the southern end of the Shenandoah Valley. Crossed by both the Blue Ridge and Appalachian ranges, this is not easy country in which to build a power line. But these Virginia farmers wanted electricity and gradually the co-operative's lines spread out across the valleys and ridges. But unfortunately Craig-Botetourt's members had been allowed to forget about the co-op and its organization once the line had been brought to the farm home. The co-op office in New Castle was little more than an address to which to send the check for the monthly bill.

Nevertheless, the co-op continued to grow, if only through the spreading demand for central station power. By 1948, Craig-Botetourt was a million-dollar business, operating over five hundred miles of line serving over fifteen hundred farmers. But this growth had brought problems, problems that seemed beyond the capacity of the Craig-Botetourt farmer-manager. There was a power shortage. There was a shortage of wire and other supplies with which to build additional line. The contact between manager and membership was virtually nonexistent and the members were never told the reasons for construction delays and power shortages. The office management was inefficient. Records were not kept up-to-date and billing procedures were faulty. Apathy and resentment had spread not only among the membership but even in the board of directors.

At about this time Craig-Botetourt's attorney approached the Appalachian Power Company with a request to buy power. The company replied that it had no surplus. In the discussion the lawyer had made it seem as though the co-op would be in a bad way if it could not find an additional source of power. This was the signal for the company to try to bring about the purchase of this very valuable property.

The approach was cleverly worked out. During the winter of 1948 the Appalachian company held cooking classes throughout the New Castle area. Farmers' wives were taught cooking, and at the same time they were instructed in the benefits of selling out to a private, efficient business-managed company. The company's rates, they were told, were lower than those of Craig-Botetourt, and besides, the company's customers were not saddled with a government debt. Why not sell out and get the benefit of proper management and lower rates? Craig-Botetourt members found in their mailboxes persuasive messages from the Appalachian president, offering to buy out the co-op for the balance of its debt to REA.

When the statewide co-op organization met in 1948, Craig-Botetourt was found to be in serious trouble. The other Virginia co-operatives voted to get together and help straighten out the New Castle office before Craig-Botetourt's annual meeting in May. Five neighboring co-ops sent eight trucks and fifty men to catch up with the applications for electrical service that had piled up. Other Virginia co-operatives sent in wire, conductors, and other materials that Craig-Botetourt had long been short of. The national association was alerted to the situation. The REA itself sent some of its crack field men to try to straighten out Craig-Botetourt and to protect the government investment there,

On the day of the annual meeting the drowsy town of New Castle, with its few stores, its courthouse and its public school, began to fill up early. The focus of interest was the co-op office in an unpretentious frame building off the main street. This was the big test of strength when the members would decide whether or not to sell their co-operative.

Both sides had been patrolling the roads leading into New Castle, asking members for their proxies either to keep or to sell the co-op. One member approached by both sides was Vice-Admiral Patrick Bellinger, who had recently retired as a naval aviator to his farm in the Virginia hills. After a long and distinguished career that included an attempt to fly the Atlantic in 1919, the battle of Pearl Harbor, and command of all naval air strength on the Atlantic seaboard, Bellinger had decided on a peaceful life as a poultry farmer.

Like so many other members, he had not paid much attention to the business of the co-op. But when he heard the arguments on both sides he said that he knew damn well that he didn't want to sell. He felt so strongly about it that he agreed to become a candidate for director on the slate that was fighting the drive by the company to take over.

It was a tense meeting. More than a thousand farmers had crowded into the high school auditorium to listen to both sides of the argument. The keynote for the co-ops was sounded by NRECA's executive manager, Clyde Ellis. Before his speech Ellis had passed out a large black book among the co-op members. This showed that the Appalachian Power Company was affiliated with the American Gas and Electric Company; that both companies had the same Wall Street address. This was the background for Ellis's fiery oratory. "Don't sell out to Wall Street interests," he pleaded. "The word of what you do here will go out in twenty-four hours to millions of farm families throughout America, and to Congress. . . . Consider not only your own welfare but that of your neighbors and fellow members everywhere. Don't surrender!" Admiral Bellinger too was a persuasive advocate for staying by the co-operative. He appealed to the farm members not to sell "their heritage for a mess of pottage."

Customarily undemonstrative, these highland farmers shouted their approval. It was apparent then that the offer of the power company would be rejected. When the debate came to an end and the vote was taken, Admiral Bellinger and the others on his slate had won by a two-to-one victory.

Since this struggle, which has become known as the Battle of New Castle, many steps have been taken to strengthen the Craig-Botetourt co-operative. A new manager was hired who set to work at once to restore efficiency. Long-delayed line construction was carried out and the sloppiness in right-of-way cutting that had formerly annoyed the farmers was eliminated. But most important of all, co-op members are no longer apathetic or indifferent. Each year nearly a thousand people attend the annual meeting at which Craig-Botetourt's progress is reviewed. Admiral Bellinger, who was elected president of the co-op, has become a leader in Virginia's rural electrification program. He is determined that his own co-op will never again fall into the sad state it was in 1948.

This is a fairly typical example of what happens when a co-op goes slack and the way seems to open up for an aggressive private utility to step in. Two power companies tried to buy out the Southeastern Michigan Rural Electric Co-operative around Adrian, Michigan. The Louisiana Power and Light Company tried to buy the South Louisiana Electric Membership Corporation. Located in the cane-brake country of Louisiana, the latter co-op had high wholesale power costs and an apathetic membership. In the Southwest, the Arizona Power Company has killed off two co-ops and unsuccessfully tried to buy out the Verde Co-operative, which had a shortage of wholesale power.

In the Sierra Nevada Mountains of California the far-spreading Pacific Gas and Electric sought to buy the Plumas Sierra Electric Co-operative. This co-op had long been plagued with low-voltage on the lines and power outages were frequent. Pacific Gas and Electric wrote the co-op directors that the company wanted to buy the whole operation. Since in California cities, the company wrote, it had as many as two hundred customers to the mile, naturally it would be able to offer Plumas Sierra's members a lower rate than they were then getting from their own co-op. The directors turned down the company's offer. Whereupon Pacific Gas and Electric went over the directors' heads and appealed to the membership. For months the giant company with all its political power and influence carried on a publicity campaign stressing the advantages of selling to a "business-managed" corporation. But the co-op defended itself successfully and finally Pacific Gas and Electric gave up.

Curiously enough, in the Northwest, where water power is so abundant and where the principle of public ownership has gained wide acceptance, several REA co-ops have had a difficult time. In Oregon and Idaho three co-operatives have been bought up, and now another, the Prairie Power Co-operative, is being tested out. The company that has been so successful in acquiring these co-operatives is the Idaho Power Company. This company, once a subsidiary of what John Gunther calls that "huge spidery octopus, the

Electric Bond and Share Company," operates in regions still served by affiliates of Bond and Share.

In general, the Idaho Power Company has done a good job of rural electrification. But for one reason or another it left large pockets without electricity. Farmers in these areas grew tired of waiting for the company to serve them and they formed their own co-ops. One of the co-operatives so formed was the Malheur Electric Co-operative with headquarters in the town of Vale, Oregon. As soon as the Malheur co-op was formed in 1939, the company began to build spite lines. One farmer has told the story of what happened as follows:

"I came to the Valley in '34. My farm was two and a half miles out of town and a half mile from the Idaho Power line but I couldn't get hooked up. Few of us could. But things changed in a hurry when we began to organize. Our line crew would set out stakes and the company would set out poles beside them. Once our boys knocked off in the evening leaving a half mile of poles standing loose in the holes. Next morning when they came to work they found their poles pushed to one side, Idaho poles set, line strung and energized right over them. At first they refused to sell us power, so forcing us to buy Diesel units . . ."

But even without the lines skimming off the most profitable business, the Idaho Company had the co-op in a vise. The handle to tighten the vise was the source of power controlled by the utility. When it was impossible to come to reasonable terms for wholesale power, with the company actually asking irrigation rates instead of wholesale rates, the co-op bought two Diesel generating units. After the generators were bought, the Idaho Company offered co-op members a wholesale rate cheaper than their generators could provide. This was possible because the company was buying cheap power from a reclamation dam. Here was an open threat to raid the membership.

Finally, in 1949, Malheur members voted to sell their power system to the utilities. This did not come, however, until after a warmly emotional contest. Older members recalled the years when they had begged the utility to give them service. They reminded younger members that in 1937, when Idaho Power had agreed to serve farmers, the price asked was an initial charge of $200 and a $6.00 minimum monthly bill. A month before the co-op was formed, this was reduced to $96 and a $5.00 minimum. And the day before farmers formed their organization, the price dropped to only $4.00 minimum charge.

Such failures are not likely in the future. One of the important activities of REA in recent years has been the building of an awareness of the value of group responsibility in a group undertaking. This was an important contribution of George W. Haggard, deputy administrator at the time of his tragic death in an airplane accident in the summer of 1951 along with other staff members of REA. As a result of his background on a Texas farm, Haggard had a deep sense of the need for understanding and education in order to bring about the participation that is essential in any co-operative undertaking.

Rural electrification today has become big and powerful. The private power companies cannot push around the larger co-operatives. And when the smaller ones are under attack, the National Rural Electric Co-operative Association comes to the rescue.

Strength has come out of union. The formation of a nationwide association was an inevitable next step. From state to state and from region to region the co-operatives vary in viewpoint, in operation, in many ways. That is one of the advantages of this decentralized approach to a national problem. Yet joined together in a national organization for certain fundamental purposes, these millions of farm families have made their voice increasingly heard.

F ORMED only ten years ago, the National Rural Electric Co-operative Association today has three million farm and other rural family members. In a decade it has become one of the most powerful farm organizations in America. While it is strictly a service organization for the electric co-ops, it ranks with such old-timers as the American Farm Bureau Federation, the Farmers' Union, and the National Grange. Both in Congress and in the country, NRECA has made itself a force widely felt.

This force stems from the grass roots of America; from farms from Maine to California on which power coming from the turn of a switch has replaced so much of the backbreaking drudgery of the past. Naturally this rapid rise has not taken place without producing resentments, jealousies, and enmities, both in the Government and in the utility industry. Utility spokesmen are fond of denouncing NRECA as the most powerful lobby in Washington. And the bureaucrats and congressmen are often resentful of the way in which the organization holds up the record and hews to the line of public and private responsibility in the framework of the REA program.

In union there is strength, and what the association has done is to protect and advance the program beginning when it was in a critical stage. Rural electrification might have been greatly curtailed without a strong and resourceful organization opposing the efforts of a large part of the utility industry to force REA to conform with the plans and intentions of the industry. Having rejected the opportunity to carry out this development, convinced of its inevitable failure, the utilities have been working hard to try to gain a position of dominance in rural, as well as in urban, America. But the distrust of the organized farmer goes very deep, and his determination to keep what he has is expressed through the NRECA.

The need of some sort of mutual protective association was evident as early as 1937. In that year John Carmody, then REA administrator, was having a bitter fight with the private power companies. They were delaying REA construction with court battles and spite lines. Carmody felt that a national association was necessary in order to present a united front to the utilities and also as a clearing house for the exchange of technical information on a wide variety of subjects. He even went so far as to reserve hotel space for a meeting of co-operative leaders to be held in Chicago at which he intended to propose the association. At the last minute Carmody changed his mind, feeling the time had not yet arrived for such an organization.

While Carmody dropped the idea, his assistant in REA, Robert Craig, did not. Traveling about the country inspecting co-operatives, Craig had a chance to talk with many farm leaders. He found almost everyone enthusiastic about a national association. Local leaders felt that they could resist the power companies' encroachments successfully only if they were organized nationally.

These talks led to discussion of the possibility of the co-operatives setting up their own mutual insurance company in order to reduce the high premiums they were paying to cover the safety of employees working on co-op lines. Others suggested that a national association could buy the materials needed by all co-ops in large quantities and thus save thousands of dollars. But in spite of this enthusiasm nothing happened. It was not until leaders in the electrification program were faced with a serious crisis that the decision was taken.

Even before Pearl Harbor in 1941, the building of REA lines came to a virtual halt. Copper and aluminum were very scarce. Defense priorities compelled the Office of Production Management (later to become the War Production Board) to issue an order sharply restricting the use of copper or aluminum in wire to construct power lines.

Not long afterward the report was circulated that a large hoard of copper wire had been found lying in a farmer's field near Gilmer, Texas. Out of this report grew the story, greatly sensationalized and elaborated upon, that REA co-operatives were hoarding scarce materials. The facts were that a contractor had bought the copper wire in Chile, intending to use it to build lines for the Upshur Rural Electric Co-operative. That was before the Government had restricted such line construction. This seemed to be a chance to discredit REA. Congress ordered an investigation which two committees carried out. The hoarding charge was found to be a figment of someone's imagination, someone obviously intent on damaging the whole electrification program.

But while the charges were proved false, co-operative leaders who had come to Washington to testify were worried. These and other attacks had created bad feeling. The program was in danger of being discredited and thereby brought to a full stop. The same necessities that had prompted the formation of statewide organizations now led inevitably to a national association.

The preliminary work previously done by Craig gave the co-operative leaders a foundation on which to build. In March of 1942, at the Willard Hotel in Washington, the National Rural Electric Co-operative Association was formed. A number of congressmen and senators attended a reception welcoming the new organization. The important role it was to play was clearly foreshadowed. At NRECA's first annual convention in St. Louis one year later official Washington from President Roosevelt on down hailed the new association.

The ten men who incorporated NRECA were grass-roots farmers, co-op managers, and rural lawyers. And they gave form to a democratic organization that has never been uprooted. Three of their number—Steve Tate of Georgia, the late E.J. Stoneman of Wisconsin, and J.C. Nichols of Wyoming—became the first presidents of the association. But only the revered "Uncle Harry" Edmunds of Minnesota still serves on NRECA's present forty-one-member board of directors.

The first task of the original incorporators was to find an executive manager. That was not at all easy. The manager would have to have extraordinary qualifications. He would have to work successfully in co-operation with the REA and with other executive departments of the Government. He would have to take an important part in standing up to the attacks of the powerful and closely knit electric power industry. Last but far from least, the manager would have to have the confidence of NRECA's farm members throughout the country. Months after the founding, NRECA President Steve Tate announced that Clyde Ellis had been chosen for the job.

Clyde Ellis comes from Arkansas, and that fact as background for his rise to national prominence tells a lot about the man. Politics in Arkansas is a hard-boiled business. Competition for every political job is tough. And an inherent almost instinctive conservatism has been deeply entrenched. It was not only that Ellis elected to go into politics, but in conservative Arkansas he was by his own choice a liberal, a New Dealer.

He had grown up on a hillside farm near Garfield, where his parents still live. There was no electricity on that farm. This energetic, intensely ambitious young man put himself through college and law school selling Bibles. An outstanding debater in college, he gravitated naturally into politics, winning a seat in the State Senate. While he was in the Arkansas Senate he introduced a bill that was to become that state's rural electrification act. His stand in favor of REA and for developing Arkansas's public power resources put him in head-on collision with what was perhaps the greatest single political force in the state. This was the Arkansas Power and Light Company and its president, C. Hamilton Moses.

Shrewd and resourceful, Moses is perfectly cast for the role he has chosen to play as "Big Man" in his state, a behind-the-scenes boss. An orator, he has an unlimited fund of stories that can captivate an audience of bankers in the city as well as the farmers gathered at the forks of the creek. That Ellis and Moses should have become bitter opponents is not surprising, since Moses has worked long and skillfully against public power and has opposed many phases of the REA program.

In spite of the determined opposition of the company, Ellis was elected to Congress in 1938. He served two terms from Arkansas's third district. But with the beginning of war a more conservative trend set in. Rural electrification and public power issues were pushed into the background. The state passed a constitutional amendment forbidding the closed shop. Even the threat of violence by labor union members was a penitentiary offense according to a law adopted in 1946. This gives some clue to the influence wielded by conservative business interests. In 1942 when Ellis ran for United States senator he was beaten in the Democratic primary. The conservative machine vote in the cities turned the tide against him.

In recognition of its rapidly growing strength, the first convention of NRECA in 1943 brought cries from the private utilities. Some charged that Roosevelt was in back of the organization as part of a plan to get rural support for a fourth term in 1944. Others saw in NRECA an instrument for the ambition of Clyde Ellis and other public power advocates. Craig was charged with impropriety for promoting such an organization while serving as deputy administrator of REA. Was there a financial motive behind all this, it was asked? Was the association planning to buy materials at wholesale or at cost for its member co-operatives, thereby short-circuiting the channels of private enterprise?

What was not evident at the first convention was the crisis that the rural power program faced from within. As a wartime measure to cut down the overcrowding in Washington, REA was now located in St. Louis. The move had caused considerable dislocation and the resignation of some of REA's officers. Harry Slattery was far from happy in the role of administrator.

A few months after the convention the St. Louis *Post-Dispatch* printed a report that NRECA was trying to have Slattery removed. The reason given was his opposition to NRECA's use of the funds of the nationwide co-operative to found two insurance companies. This marked the beginning of a dispute that had some unfortunate consequences.

The desire to reduce high insurance rates had been one of the primary motives for the formation of the national association. Shortly after its incorporation the association had started both a fire and a casualty insurance scheme. Plans for NRECA's insurance program were well advanced. Several insurance experts within REA had helped to get that program going. But when Slattery heard that the association proposed to use funds in surplus, representing an accumulation of payments by co-operative members above the amounts necessary to repay government loans, he issued a stop-look-listen letter. This letter warned the co-operatives to wait until the Department of Agriculture had passed on the legality of such an insurance program.

The legal opinion finally issued by the Department of Agriculture was indecisive. It left the matter to the discretion of the Secretary of Agriculture and the administrator of REA. Slattery held that the co-operatives could not use their surplus funds to go into the insurance business. This brought him in immediate conflict with the leaders of NRECA, who for their part thought that they had already obtained the approval of the Rural Electrification Administration for their project.

The board of NRECA authorized an indignant letter to the Secretary of Agriculture saying that the plan for the insurance companies was too far advanced to abandon. Slattery refused to alter his decision. The dispute became more or less an open feud in which a great many bitter things were said. It ended with Slattery's resignation. As investigator, planner, and critic, Slattery had, for thirty-five years, contributed much as a servant of Government. But he was miscast in the role of REA administrator and frequently found himself in unhappy controversy.

In the airing of this conflict the enemies of REA saw an opportunity. A Senate investigation was initiated. The investigating committee was dominated by a Republican, Henrik Shipstead, of Minnesota, with a Democrat, Ellitson "Cotton-Ed" Smith of South Carolina seconding him whenever it was necessary. As so often with Senate investigations, most of the effort was devoted to trying to prove conclusions that had already been reached. The inquiry might have served a real purpose if there had been an objective examination of the whole problem of the use of co-operatve funds for insurance companies by NRECA.

All this occurred, of course, in an election year when headlines based on sensationalized hearings were thought to be useful in discrediting Roosevelt and all that he stood for. Because he would not reveal private conversations he had with the President, the committee counsel threatened Jonathan Daniels, one of Roosevelt's aides, with a contempt citation. Daniels' position was upheld when the committee decided that a presidential assistant could not be forced to reveal his conversations with the Chief Executive. This was about the only tangible result produced by the Senate investigation.

The fire and casualty companies that had been incorporated by NRECA in Maryland were abandoned. Lengthy negotiations were held with several private insurance companies. Belief was widespread that rural electrification had not existed sufficiently long enough to establish safe construction and maintenance procedures. And this viewpoint was undoubtedly colored by the notion that farmers banded together in locally owned co-ops were incapable of running an electric power company.

The association at last reached an agreement with the Employers' Mutual, a Wausau, Wisconsin, firm. This company agreed to cut the premiums for liability insurance by twenty-five per cent, where it was allowable, in return for the large volume of business to be provided through NRECA. The company also cut the cost of fidelity bonds in view of the small loss suffered by co-operatives through dishonest employees. Besides cutting rates, the firm agreed to employ a safety engineer who would work with the co-ops.

In many respects this was the least of REA's problems at this critical period. The fine reputation that had been built up by the Administration was harmed. Charges of corruption brought up during the Shipstead investigation left an unpleasant aftermath, even though those charges were proven baseless. The NRECA suffered too. Many of the co-ops were distressed that their association had gotten into such a controversy. As a result membership fell off for several years afterward.

But with the combined efforts of a new administrator, Claude Wickard, who had been Secretary of Agriculture during the Slattery regime, and Clyde Ellis, the damage that had been done was overcome. Today the Rural Electrification Administration and NRECA work closely together to solve the problems facing the rural power co-operatives.

Certainly the most pressing problem before the REA co-operatives today is the ever increasing need for abundant low-cost power. As the co-ops face heavier and heavier demands for electricity, the cost of such power becomes a larger and larger item in the budget. And what is more, as the co-operatives reach out to serve thinner and thinner territory, the necessity for low-cost power becomes imperative. When the utilities cannot supply the volume of power at a price the co-operatives can afford to pay, the co-ops seek either to build their own generating stations, or to tie in with lines bringing hydroelectricity generated at federal dams if it is available. The commercial power companies are determined to keep control of the source of power that energizes REA lines. They bitterly attack the loans made to the co-operatives for the purpose of building steam-generating plants. The companies each year bring pressure on Congress to cut appropriations for public transmission lines with which to transmit federally generated power.

The NRECA has fought just as hard for these appropriations. NRECA has supported appropriations for Bonneville, the Southwestern Power Administration, the Southeastern Power Administration, the Bureau of Reclamation projects, and TVA. NRECA's farm leaders consider the arguments of the power companies that REA is seeking to duplicate existing facilities and to build up a public power empire with which to destroy private utilities merely part of the attempt to monopolize the distribution of power generated at federal dams. "What nonsense it is," says Ellis, "to talk of REA co-ops putting private power companies out of business when co-operative electric systems actually get less than five per cent of federally generated power."

Each year when Congress considers the plans of the Department of the Interior to distribute power generated at federal dams, with preference under law to rural systems and municipalities, NRECA members from all parts of the country come before House and Senate committees to present the case for the co-ops. In 1949 more than a hundred spokesmen from the farms joined in asking for funds for the Southwestern Power Administration. The following year so many co-op officers wanted to testify before the Senate that each was allowed to talk for only five minutes.

With a sense of urgency these co-operative leaders argued that kilowatts developed by federal investment should be sold on a pay-as-you-go basis to agencies having a public interest greater than that of the private power companies. After all, these farmers asked, whose power is it? In the course of the hearings they raised what is another bone of contention—whether there are power shortages around the country. Ernest Wood of Chillicothe, Missouri, told the Senate in 1950 that his co-operative was facing power shortages and that the local power company was wrong when it said there was plenty of power. R.J. Martin of the Boone Electric Co-operative of Columbia, Missouri, said, "There is definitely a power shortage in Missouri; ask the farmers, they know about it."

Ellis backs up these co-operative directors and managers. He points out that the Missouri, Arkansas, Oklahoma area is known as a power desert. "The reason why this area has a low national average in rural electrification," says Ellis, "is because the co-operatives haven't a sufficient supply of low-cost power."

The private utility companies challenge such statements. Their spokesmen contradict co-operative officers. The companies deny Bureau of Reclamation officials who talk about the need for low-cost power to be distributed to REA systems. The companies even deny the figures of the Federal Power Commission, which showed that in 1949 nearly one half of the nation's power systems were compelled to reduce their loads. But the co-ops know from actual experience. They have repeatedly come up against restrictions on the amount of power that can be sold to any one customer, as well as actual shortages. So they are fearful of complete dependence on the commercial power companies. As Clyde Ellis puts it, "The co-op boys just do not control their life line and they are scared and uneasy. They realize that when they sit down with the power companies to bargain for wholesale power it is not on an equal basis."

NRECA's board and repeated resolutions adopted by delegates in convention marshal some powerful arguments to convince Congress that it is necessary to continue to provide loans to build generating and transmission units. They point out that the use of electricity on the farm is fast outstripping available supplies of electricity. In a five-year period during the forties, the use of farm power purchased from private utilities quadrupled. This is a measure of how rapidly the hired hand is being replaced by the electric hand. Co-operative after co-operative complain that the private companies supplying their power can no longer fill their needs. Farmers on co-operative systems are becoming more and more uneasy, and this uneasiness is reflected in a growing number of applications for loans with which to build generating plants, or for transmission lines to connect with federal hydro power.

The arguments raised against these loans by the private utilities become more insistent, franker, seeming to indicate a growing confidence that this stage of the program can be stopped entirely. Frank Wilkes, president of the Southwestern Gas and Electric Company, called plans to build REA generating plants "foolish and unnecessary expenditures." "We strongly recommend," he said to a committee of Congress, "that proper safeguards be placed in this and other appropriation bills to insure that funds not be wasted in harebrained projects and useless duplications of existing facilities."

Recognizing that the generation program is the main objective of the power industry's attack, militant resolutions approved by co-op delegates have repeatedly assailed this point of view. If ever, they tell Congress, the right of the co-ops to build their own generating plants is taken away, the whole REA program will be in trouble. Time after time again in Virginia, Texas, North Carolina, Iowa, Wisconsin, and Arkansas, private companies have cut their rates, sometimes by half, when a co-operative, after long and futile bargaining for low-cost power, has applied for a generating loan. The ability of the co-ops to build their own generating plants is a measure of competition. This competition, it is argued, keeps power company rates down. And one of the more farm-minded utility executives, Grover Neff of the Wisconsin Power and Light Company, speaking for the conservative Edison Electric Institute in 1945, admitted that REA competition had been "a booster of activity"; that it had put the power industry on its mettle.

Malcolm Wehrung, a former REA lawyer, effectively summed up the co-operative point of view on this perennial dispute over the right to generate electricity. He put it thus: "An electric distribution system without control over its energy supply is like an automobile without a motor, a cart without a horse, or a farm without a plow. The owner of such an automobile, farm, or cart is entirely dependent upon his neighbors for the useful operation of his own properties. If the neighbors are unfriendly and have the reputation for overcharging or for charging all the traffic will bear, then the farmer will be determined to obtain for his own use the absolute essentials." As Wehrung saw it, the electric co-operatives have no alternative.

A major test on this issue is yet to come. Administrator Wickard believes the attitude of the commercial utilities is still that of a sovereign power determined to keep out of their province interlopers such as power co-operatives. According to Wickard, the industry still seems to consider it "presumptuous for a group of farmers to engage in business, other than tilling the soil, the object of which is to supply themselves with a vital necessity of life." If the showdown comes on what so many farm co-operators believe to be the essential factor in the growth and survival of what they have built, then NRECA will be in the forefront of the struggle.

One of the immediate concerns of the association is to be sure that official Washington knows how its three million farm members feel about the attempts of "economy-minded" congressmen, who claim that rural electrification is completed and therefore call for a cutback in the REA program. In 1935 the electric utilities found there were very few farms requiring electric service that were not already served. In 1945 Grover Neff and other utility executive were telling Congress that the rural electrification program was just about finished. Neff testified that REA had enough money to complete the job of electrifying America's farms. REA at that time had three hundred million dollars on hand.

"If REA will spend three hundred million dollars in the next three years," Neff said, "and if the utilities will spend nearly as much, the job of extending service to the farms of this country will be approximately at an end."

Clyde Ellis appeared before the same committee to refute Neff and his contention that rural electrification was virtually completed. Ellis presented detailed figures in answer, showing that there would still be one and a half million farms without electricity when REA's loaning capacity at that point was exhausted. Ellis put before the committee resolutions endorsed by half a million farmers calling for funds to complete REA's work. Congress was persuaded, and voted for the appropriations.

Lobbyist and demagogue are two of the mildest epithets applied to Ellis by the private power industry. They are a tribute to his effectiveness in forging a protective ring around the co-operatives. If Ellis has been effective in protecting the co-operatives, it is no accident, for long before he was selected as manager of the association he realized the need for mutual protection and wrote of that need to leaders in the power program.

With his powerful voice, his flailing gestures, his big balding head, Ellis is an impressive figure on the platform. After the rough and tumble of his experience in Arkansas politics, he knows the language that is understood by the big farm audiences assembled under the blazing sun in Iowa, Alabama, or almost anywhere else in the forty-eight United States. He is a kind of fireman too, ready to rush out to the aid of a threatened co-operative. A fighter, he does not mind getting into trouble when that seems to be necessary. The struggle to save the Craig-Botetourt Co-operative in Virginia illustrated that.

The most insidious attack directed at the REA co-ops has come from the National Tax Equality Association. This resourceful organization, purporting to be composed of small businessmen, has lobbied persistently to get Congress to pass legislation placing a discriminatory tax on co-operatives. Literature has been widely distributed, including cartoons appearing in many newspapers and magazines, picturing co-ops as enjoying their "tax-free" rides on the backs of businessmen.

NRECA hits right back at the Tax Equality Association. They point out that a substantial amount of its support comes from large corporations, among them power companies. Again and again NRECA officials and other leaders in the American co-operative movement have appeared before Congress to point out the difference between profits and capital payments to members. They have explained before a number of congressional committees that REA co-ops pay all local and state taxes that a commercial power company does.

Ellis, his staff, and the farm leaders behind them bring to rural electrification a devotion so intense that it is almost religious in nature. Ellis's drive, coming from many sources in his own background, is the mainspring in NRECA's struggle in behalf of its members. Two and a half months of every year he devotes to visiting individual co-operatives and attending regional meetings. A day on the road begins early in the morning at some airport. Then follows a drive to the meeting, a speech to deliver, shaking hands, lunch, and afterwards lengthy discussions of problems facing the region.

When addressing a crowd gathered at an annual co-op rally he sometimes reminds his listeners of the revivalist. He speaks with fervor and passion. Lashing out at the Wall Street crowd, and the eastern money interests, he tips his head back, his eyes close, and his hands chop the air to emphasize a point against the "profit utilities."

In 1950 the Farmers' Union presented Ellis with an award for his "outstanding service to agriculture." Recalling his efforts as state legislator, as congressman, and presently as manager of NRECA in behalf of the rural power program, the award states that Ellis "has worked vigorously to improve the living conditions of farm people." Considering the work and responsibilities that he shoulders, by Washington standards for such a job he is modestly rewarded. The $16,000 a year he is paid is small compared with the $65,000 salary of Purcell Smith, who represented the leading commercial utilities association.

NRECA's job is never finished. In the years ahead, as the rural power program faces determined opposition, the stocky figure of Clyde Ellis, his piercing gray eyes shaded by a Stetson tilted a little forward, may well possess the key to success or failure.

Holding the line for the REA program is only part of NRECA's job. It acts as a clearing house for information, publishing each month an excellent trade magazine edited by William Roberts. And it handles the insurance program of member co-operatives wishing to take advantage of it services.

REA co-ops had, at the outset at least, a personnel problem. They were unable to compete in salaries with the private utilities. And there was the problem of employee pensions. A co-op employing fifteen or twenty people found it difficult or impossible to provide an adequate retirement plan, again in competition with the private utilities which had in many instances led the way in establishing employee pension systems. NRECA evolved a plan on a nationwide basis under which every co-operative employee can have the security of a pension and welfare benefits.

Since 1947, Harry Edmunds of Minnesota, one of the grand old men of the rural electrification movement, has worked to promote this retirement system. He stresses its value in building morale and efficiency and consequently in establishing a permanent staff. He also reminds farmers of the gratitude they owe their linemen, engineers, and managers.

"How much will be my satisfaction," Edmunds has written, "in knowing on a stormy night when the lineman is out bucking the elements and is doing his best to restore service, that I have done a little to repay him for that particular part of the service he is rendering; for accepting as part of his duty the hardships he is encountering."

One of the most valuable services that NRECA performed for its member co-ops was to solve the shortage of aluminum wire that from 1946 until 1949 was slowing up the program. In breaking this bottleneck of supply, the NRECA proved the usefulness of a national association which could co-ordinate the efforts of all rural electric co-ops.

Aluminum was scarce for many reasons. Foremost was the shortage of electricity, which is used in enormous quantities in aluminum production. Before full-scale rearmament began in 1940, the industry had been unable to expand gradually to meet the demand for wire by rural power systems. Faced with the demand that had accumulated during the war, deliveries were promised four years after orders were placed. Meanwhile some twenty thousand miles of co-operative poles were standing idle, waiting for the conductor with which to carry electricity to thousands of farmhouses.

Working closely with REA, the national association approached the Reynolds Metal Company with an order that would guarantee the metal company a large market for many years to come. One agent, the Wisconsin Electric Co-operative, was to purchase the conductor from the Reynolds Company. The Wisconsin co-operative was picked because, as purchasing agent for many Wisconsin co-ops, it had had experience in dealing with large amounts of material. Acceptance of this contract by the aluminum company broke the bottleneck. When, in addition, the NRECA helped to find a source of power for Reynolds's Arkansas aluminum plant, the shortage disappeared.

Copper and aluminum prices dropped sharply as other metal manufacturers bid for the huge REA market. Companies that one day had announced a year's wait for delivery of aluminum conductor, the next day found they could supply the needs of the co-operatives immediately. Key to this problem was the close working arrangement between the co-ops functioning through NRECA and REA.

In 1949 NRECA held its convention in New York City. Four thousand delegates from forty-two states and Alaska came to the big town. It was a memorable meeting between the grass roots of America and the sidewalks of the largest city in the world. New York was impressed. The *Herald Tribune* wrote that this was truly rural America. Rural electrification had come of age in an impressive fashion.

The organization operates through the democratic process. Each co-operative elects a delegate to the state, regional, and national meetings. The delegates of each state elect a director on the national board. These state directors, either farm members or active in farm work, meet twice a year to determine the policy of the association in Washington. There is also a ten-man executive committee of the national board. The states are divided into ten regions and in each of these regions the states elect from their several directors of the national board an executive committeeman.

Men like Harry Edmunds, the late E.J. Stoneman of Wisconsin, John George from Idaho, Clyde Seybold from Indiana, Steve Tate from Georgia, Clark McWhorter from Oklahoma, Tom Craddock from Texas, Harry Nuttle from Maryland, have guided the policies of NRECA. They have helped to correct the mistakes of the first years.

The quality of the leadership is one of the forces that have made NRECA strong. They are big men, big physically, unmistakably American in lineament, voice, gesture, important in their respective communities. Steve Tate is of the Tates of Tate, Georgia. E.J. Stoneman played a leading role in both education and politics in Wisconsin. J.C. Nichols's story is the characteristic American saga of the poor boy who became a millionaire through his own efforts. Tom Craddock and Clark McWhorter both have in their bearing and their manner the friendliness and the independence of the Southwest; they would have led in any field in which they had chosen to work. These are the men who have built NRECA, serving at a sacrifice of endless time in various offices, including the top one.

Ellis takes no policy steps without the approval of the executive committee. The committee travels to Washington four or five times a year to make major decisions and to review what has been taking place. They donate their time to the national association, as do many hundreds of other "volunteers" who are the real backbone of the rural power program. They are not all agreed on policy. Some of them would like to see the fight with the commercial companies ended. As one of them put it, "We've got the same interests; if we both set to work there's enough work to keep everybody busy for the next twenty years. We're the companies' best customers and we're buying more power from them every year."

Others, and probably the majority, feel that the co-ops' only salvation is to build up independent sources of rural power and they believe it should be done in part through linking up with federally owned transmission lines, federal hydroelectric power projects and, in part, through the establishment of far more steam-generating plants. These are the men who feel there is no way around the bitterness, the implacable opposition, that has come out of the long conflict.

NRECA is a force that cannot be ignored either in Washington or in the country. The strong sinews of three million farm families are woven into it. When their representatives in Congress vote on an REA measure, that vote is carefully tabulated by NRECA and the record of it spread far and wide. Special interests? Pressure groups? Yes, your farm co-operator will answer. But it happens that when we speak it is for a lot of people and not just for a few companies. That is why our voice is heard and we mean to go on making it heard.

IN MAY OF 1951, REA celebrated its sixteenth birthday with a traditional birthday dinner in Washington. These are likely to be rather routine occasions with everyone making flattering speeches about everyone else. But this time the principal speaker was Senator Paul Douglas of Illinois, who almost always has something to say.

Senator Douglas talked about the disease of adminstrativeitis as it afflicts government agencies in Washington. He described two forms of this creeping paralysis. Regulatory agencies are especially subject to the first form of this disease which results in the agency being gradually taken over by the interests it is charged with regulating. Finally it becomes difficult to tell the agency from the special interest. As an example, the senator cited the Interstate Commerce Commission, which seems to exist chiefly to ratify decisions already taken by the railroads and the bus lines. A second form of administrativeitis, according to Douglas, is just plain atrophy and decay. Looking down at the well-fed diners, most of them from REA, the senator from Illinois with a quizzical smile on his face wondered whether REA had escaped the blight of administrativeitis.

If performance is any test, then the answer must be yes. Unlike the Interstate Commerce Commission, REA is not a regulatory body. It was created to administer a lending service to the farmers of America. Its principal role is that of a banker to farmers wishing to supply themselves with electric power. But when REA has made a loan it both supervises and encourages its borrower to become a successful business. This has meant inevitably that the identity of interests between the agency and those it serves has been close. The present administrator, Claude Wickard, is guided by the needs of the farmers for whom REA was created.

The fourth administrator of REA, Wickard is the first one who was himself a dirt farmer. He still owns and supervises the operation of a big farm in Carroll County, Indiana, which has been in the Wickard family for four generations. And he is a member of the Carroll County Rural Electric Membership Corporation, which serves his farm with electric power. A stocky, broad-shouldered man with a somewhat humorous expression on his face, Wickard, despite his years in Washington, still looks like a son of the soil. He is quite a different cut from the scholarly engineer, Morris Cooke, or the bluff, hard-driving Carmody, or the unhappy, retiring Slattery. Even in the midst of a serious conference of REA co-op leaders, the dirt farmer from Indiana has the air of just having got off the tractor. He has helped to guide REA through a transition period and into a more mature phase of its development.

But those who have been at the top would be the first to say that the success of REA is in large measure due to a devotion and zeal that run through the rank and file. Lawyers, engineers, co-operative organizers have worked long and hard through the years to make REA a success. They have taken the co-operative systems off the drawing boards, translating plants into reality and thereby bringing the benefits of electricity to millions of farm people. Often the clash of ideas and philosophies within REA has been violent. On occasion each administrator has been hard put to it to contain these quarrels within the agency. But these were disagreements not on the goal to be reached but on how to reach the goal.

It was Morris Cooke who first introduced, and Carmody who carried out, the techniques of management and engineering. Cooke brought into REA men like Harlow Person and Colonel George Babcock, widely recognized as experts in their field. These men set up a production system within a matter of days where formerly it took at least six months. They made lawyers, engineers, and auditors become part of a production line, with each man allotted so much time in which to finish his individual work. And if the work was not finished on schedule, the laggards were called to account.

As to the actual driving power behind the program, Carmody believed it came from the farm men and women. Their need—yes, their demand—for electricity gave rise to a missionary spirit that has marked not a little of REA's work. Without this driving force a program could never have been advanced so far in so short a time.

The job of building the lines and devising a management system for the co-ops was the work of Carmody. He instituted production conferences soon after he took over from Cooke as administrator. His conferences are still remembered by old hands in the agency. Carmody's Irish wit and sarcasm would fill the whole building with laughter. At those conferences there was only one criterion—how many lines had been built. Lawyers, engineers, and utilization people would report on each phase of every project and every application.

At first Carmody found that there was a violent dispute between a group favoring loans to co-ops and another group skeptical as to the ability of a co-operative to run an electric power business. This was an honest difference of opinion, but it was one that had to be settled before anything else could be done. Carmody recalls how this quarrel broke out at his first production meeting and he says, "We never had another. We settled the issues then and there, threw the hatchet out the window and really began to build lines instead of talk and argue." Speaking from time to time out in the country, he could be counted on for rough-hewn humor that made his point. He told a group of farm co-operators in Fort Dodge, Iowa: "I don't know anything about utility rates. But I know that they're too damned high."

It has been said that Carmody was heavy-handed with both the power companies and the co-operatives, but these critics of later years failed to understand the intensity of the fight with the power companies that Carmody was forced to wage. Senator Norris wrote Roosevelt in 1939 that Carmody had been "in a bitter fight with the power companies from the moment he had assumed his present position, and I doubt very much whether you are acquainted, except in a general way, with the details of the fight he has been compelled to carry on." As soon as a project had been processed through REA and the loan approved, the co-op would find its market raided by private companies. Then there were long wrangles with the private utility, often carried on before state public utility commissions, over a reasonable rate for wholesale power. Sometimes it was not until the co-op threatened to build its own generating plant that rates could be agreed upon. Unless Carmody had used the utmost power granted him by Congress, rural electrification would hardly have made the progress that it did.

One of the obstacles he faced was the lack of legal precedent for electric co-operatives. Prior to 1935, only one state, Iowa, had an express statutory provision for distribution of electric power through a co-operative association. About half the states had laws to cover agricultural marketing co-ops, but these statutes were not satisfactory for the needs of the REA co-operatives. REA lawyers were therefore compelled to write a new book of co-operative law.

Another important legal question was whether the co-ops were public utilities. This had to be settled according to the laws of each of the forty-eight states. There were states such as Virginia that declared the co-operatives to be public utilities so they would have to operate under the jurisdiction of the state regulatory commission. And since these commissions were more often than not biased in favor of the private utilities, this put an additional handicap on the co-ops.

Another legal obstacle was the right-of-way program. Utility corporations have the right to set up their poles along the highways of the states. They also have the right of eminent domain, allowing them to run their power lines across a farm property, with, of course, due compensation to the owners. Since the co-ops took the stand that they were not public utilities, they could not claim the right of eminent domain, and in many states they were refused the right to set up poles along country roads. Besides, the co-ops, with their slim budgets, had to design their systems to follow the most direct path, which was not usually along twisting roads. Therefore it became necessary to secure voluntary easements across the fields of individual farmers. In Carmody's administration nearly a million such easements were obtained. Some farmers objected to having poles set up on their property. They got in the way of plowing. Or they were regarded as likely to attract lightning and therefore to create an added hazard for stock in the fields.

Still another legal obstacle was interference caused on rural telephone wires by the co-operatives' high voltage power lines. Rural telephone companies frequently found it necessary to rebuild their lines in order to get rid of the buzzing caused by a nearby high tension line. So the telephone companies—and often there were scores of small mutual companies within a single co-op's area—brought suit to force the co-operative to pay for changing over the telephone lines. If the decision had gone against the co-ops, they would have been bankrupt. But fortunately in most states the courts held that the fault lay with the telephone companies' ancient lines which were not properly grounded. In view of all this and many other problems—insurance, railway, and highway crossings—it is easy to see how heavy was the burden on REA's legal staff. Thirty-five separate legal documents were necessary for each loan that was approved. No wonder Harry Slattery wrote that REA had "virtually created a new body of law"!

In many areas the very idea of a co-operative was strange. There was little realization of the time and the energy, the dedication and the devotion, that would have to come from individual members if the co-operative was to be built soundly so that it could survive in good times and bad. And the continuing pressure to get on with the job made it difficult and sometimes impossible to proceed with sufficient care and deliberation.

From the farms came a mounting chorus of impatience as word spread of what electricity could do in transforming farm life. One farmer wrote that if REA did not get around soon to helping him electrify his farm, he intended to go into the business of raising lightning bugs. Haste was imperative, too, in many areas where the power companies were moving in to skim off the best of the business with only the less prosperous farms left for the co-ops. Under Carmody, field organizers were sent out to establish direct relationships between the Administration in Washington and the co-operatives around the country. He felt strongly that such a relationship with the borrower was a healthy one. Direct dealing was, he felt, preferable to allowing an intermediary to grow up, as in Indiana, where the Farm Bureau rendered statewide engineering and purchasing services for all electric co-ops. In 1938 Carmody wrote a co-op leader that he believed "one of the real dangers of the program is that professional people hired to do a technical job for borrowers will run it to suit themselves."

This does not mean, of course, that REA sought to prevent the co-operatives from forming state or regional organizations to protect and preserve their interests in that way. The growth of state associations, and eventually of a national organization, was welcomed by REA. But each co-op still maintains direct relations with the agency in Washington.

One responsibility keenly felt by REA was the encouragement of the greatest possible use of electricity on the farm. Only in that way would the farmer get the most out of the time and the money he was investing in bringing electricity to his place. Someone in REA must have remembered the traveling circus that the Boston Edison Company had used at the turn of the century to promote the use of electric power. For in 1938 there appeared REA's "circus," officially called the Farm Depression Tour. To the children of small towns in Iowa and Nebraska it must have seemed indeed as though the circus had come to town. In would roll a procession of big trucks, one truck carrying a large tent and the others refrigerators, ensilage cutters, hay dryers, electric stoves, and other equipment, large and small. The tent would be set up in a field near the town and the circus would begin.

Sometimes as many as five thousand people a day came from neighboring counties to see the exhibit. Inside the tent a local women's organization would prepare hot meals for all visitors, using electricity to show how life in the kitchen could be simplified. In the field, the farm men would watch hammer mills, corn shellers, or pig brooders being demonstrated. The high point of the three-day exhibition was a cooking contest on the closing night between several farmers, which both entertained and instructed the audience.

These tours were highly successful. Country newspapers devoted whole editions to the circus and the REA program. Farmers skeptical as to the value of electricity were encouraged to join a local cooperative. While REA's circus toured only a few years, it gave an impetus to the promotion of power use that has been felt ever since. Annual co-op meetings almost always feature displays and demonstrations of electrical equipment. This is manufactured, and in almost all instances sold, through the channels of private enterprise. Many co-ops have found it profitable to employ home economists and agricultural engineers to show farm members how they can benefit from new uses of electricity.

Through the years and leading up to the war the program forged ahead. In 1937 there were 120 systems, in 1938, 360 systems. By the end of 1939 nearly two hundred thousand miles of line had been built, serving nearly a half a million consumers. Carmody had begun to apply mass-production techniques to line building. Battleship construction, a pole with cross arms, had given place to the slim strong poles commonly shorn of cross arms and uncluttered with useless hardware and gadgets. Span lengths had been nearly doubled as

REA engineers borrowed the best construction practices from nearly every source. Farm people were overjoyed at seeing the poles, marching across the countryside. A Texas rancher wrote the administrator:

"I have been in various parts of Texas where there have been oil booms, where enthusiasm was at fever heat, where it cost two dollars a plate for ham and eggs, and where one was glad to pay five dollars to spend one night in a barber chair. But I have never seen such enthusiasm as is now shown in Deaf Smith and Castro counties over the coming of REA electricity."

When Roosevelt decided in 1939 to place REA within the Department of Agriculture, Carmody quit in protest. The President's aim was to cut down on the number of independent agencies which had grown during the early years of the New Deal. The idea was to simplify the structure of the Government so that there would be far fewer bureaus reporting directly to the White House. But Carmody was opposed to intervention in any way with the skilled, highly efficient organization he had built up. Also he felt that the Department of Agriculture was too political in nature. He was not the only one to oppose the change. Senator Norris wrote the President a strong letter of protest expressing his fears that the whole rural electrification program, which he called one of the brightest spots in Roosevelt's administration, would be injured. Slattery, then in the Department of the Interior, is said to have opposed the shift, as did Clyde Ellis, later to become executive manager of the National Rural Electric Co-operative Association.

Whether the move was actually harmful, it is difficult to say. At about the same time other events occurred which were far more unsettling in their effect on REA. Drafted to fill the vacant post as REA administrator, Slattery was almost from the first uneasy in his new role. The war brought a sharp contest for scarce materials. As defense agencies fought for space in overcrowded Washington, REA was ordered moved to St. Louis, and in the course of the move lost many of its ablest technicians, engineers, and production experts who were drafted into defense planning or the armed services. A feud between Slattery and his deputy, Robert Craig, was finally aired in a congressional hearing.

Under the pressure of the most devastating war in history, the contribution made by REA was even more apparent than it had been in peacetime. The drain of manpower from the farms of America threatened the production of food and agricultural raw materials, which were as essential to the war effort as planes and tanks. At the same time Claude Wickard, then Secretary of Agriculture, outlined a task for the farmer overwhelming in scope. Production of many crops and livestock, he said, had to be increased as much as twenty-five per cent. Wickard called for the production of thirteen billion pounds of hogs, one hundred and twenty-eight billion pounds of milk, and four billion pounds of chickens. Besides this, Wickard wrote, the farmer was expected to harvest fifty-two million acres of wheat, eighty-eight million acres of corn, twenty-three million acres of cotton, and also to cut thirty-three million board feet of lumber. With the acute shortage of farm labor, these production goals could never have been met without the help of electric power.

The electric milking machine enabled an Iowa farmer who had lost his three hired men to the war to continue to produce twenty-five thousand quarts of milk a year. It was electricity that allowed Daniel Flinn in Illinois to run his one-hundred-and-twenty-acre farm without help. Flinn found that the electric pump saved an hour's labor in watering hogs each day, and the electric brooder made it possible for him to double his hog production. The War Production Board, seeing the value of electric power to farm production, lifted its ban on line building materials in 1942. If a farmer had ten or more animals on hand, and if the cost of bringing the power line to his farm was not more than $1500, he could be hooked up to lines where power was available. But in some regions power shortages had already begun to develop.

Not until after the controversy within REA had gone on for more than a year did Slattery resign. That was in November of 1944. President Roosevelt nominated for the vacant post of administrator Aubrey Williams, who had held various positions in the New Deal. The Senate refused to confirm the nomination.

When Harry Truman became President in April of 1945, the members of the cabinet followed the usual custom and offered their resignations. Wickard for one was anxious to resign and go back home to Indiana. He had been in Washington since 1933 and he was tired. But the new President, seeking someone with knowledge and experience, prevailed upon the retiring Secretary of Agriculture to become REA administrator. Looking back on it, Wickard says that no other government job could possibly have persuaded him to stay on in the capital. His first task was, of course, to get line building started again. The pent-up demand for power on the farms was still very great. Applications for nearly a quarter of a billion dollars in new lines and generating equipment had accumulated in the files of REA during the war. On the basis of these applications, the agency drew up a detailed five-year program.

The Congress, fearing a postwar depression, was looking for projects that would help take up the expected slack in the nation's economy. Co-operative leaders, ably represented by the NRECA, impressed upon Congress the need for and the benefits that would result from an accelerated rural power program. So despite the power companies, who appeared in force to testify that "rural electrification was virtually completed" and hence there was no need for further appropriations. REA received sufficient money. However, materials were still in short supply.

For instance, there was a serious shortage of poles. REA engineers told pole producers that they would need some twelve million poles during the first three postwar years, and two million poles a year thereafter. As early as 1940, when line building exceeded a hundred thousand miles a year, shortages had begun to develop. With the war's end pole suppliers were unable to meet even a fraction of REA's needs. Here again the co-operatives themselves, working through their national association, were able to lend a hand in breaking this bottleneck. In Texas a group of co-operatives purchased a pole creosoting plant, thus relieving an acute local shortage. Meanwhile J. C. Nichols, one of the founders and at that time president of NRECA, brought to bear his knowledge of the lumber business. A colorful personality who had been a friend of Indian scout Buffalo Bill Cody, a wrestler, hunter, and rancher, Nichols was also one of the world's largest manufacturers of veneer. He flew around the country, urging pole suppliers to expand their production.

After conferences between REA, the Forest Service, the Reconstruction Finance Corporation, and fifteen large pole suppliers, it was decided to develop the yellow pine wood lots of the South and the lodgepole pine forests of the Rocky Mountains to a much greater extent. Pole suppliers began to expand their production. They installed mechanical pole peelers. And when coal strikes in the immediate postwar years made creosote scarce, creosote was replaced as a preservative by a new chemical, pentachlorophenol. And finally new enterprises came into existence. Gradually, through the combined efforts of the Government and the co-ops, the bottleneck was broken.

By 1947 the building program was so far along that two houses were being connected each minute of every working day. Yet Wickard found pockets developing within the co-operatives in which farms were without electricity. These farmers complained that some co-ops refused to extend their lines to reach the most remote farmhouses, just as in another day that same complaint had been brought against the power companies. This brought up the old problem of area coverage, the conviction of every administrator beginning with Morris Cooke that to be successful rural electrification must cover whole areas, and not follow certain limited favorable routes. But the co-operative directors and managers, having worked hard to build their systems into financially sound enterprises, were reluctant to gamble financial success by expanding into ever thinner and thinner territory.

Representative Stephen Pace of Georgia several years earlier had introduced a bill to encourage these co-operatives to serve areas in which the returns would inevitably be smaller. Pace had drafted his bill after lengthy conferences with co-op leaders who explained the difficulties of reaching isolated farm sections. The Pace Act, which passed Congress in 1944, lowered the interest rate on REA loans and gave the co-ops a longer time in which to repay the principal. Still they were slow in expanding. Wickard read co-operative leaders a lecture on the need to go all the way so that there would not be "dark spots in the rural economy, both literally and figuratively." Today the co-ops are for the most part following the principle of area coverage which is basic to the whole program.

Quite apart from the physical undertaking, formidable as that was, there were other problems almost equally complicated and difficult. Co-operative education had lagged behind. Many co-op members, particularly in the South and the West where the concept was comparatively new, understood little about the management of their co-op's affairs or the necessity of keeping a watchful eye over their own enterprise. The tendency was to leave the welfare of their self-owned business up to the board of directors, the manager, or the REA itself. This made for laxity and indifference, and in some instances it was an invitation to power companies that saw an opportunity to acquire a going and prosperous business at a portion of its original cost.

Along with this went the continual harassment of commercial utility propaganda intended to intimidate farm co-operators. The program was called socialistic. The superiority of "business-managed" commercial enterprise was held as a contrast. Too often farmers failed to realize that the bills they were paying for electric power also included an amount for repayment of the debt their co-operative owed to the Government. Farmers many times forgot that the Government had supplied virtually all the money invested in their co-ops. This 100-per-cent loan financing, a unique feature of the REA program, was necessary if the farmer was to be able to undertake rural electrification. It meant, however, that the REA co-ops, unlike other businesses, had to retire the entire investment in their enterprise. Farmers who were repaying this investment little by little did not always understand that, as the government loan was repaid, they were becoming outright owners of the poles and lines that made up their system.

One of Wickard's aims, working closely with the NRECA, has been to encourage a wider understanding of the co-operative concept and the necessity for continuing leadership for steady, sound development. This has not always been easy. Crosscurrents of opinion, representing regional differences and prejudices, have at times made for conflict. One difference has been over how ultimate ownership of the co-op system is to be distributed.

During the early years of the REA program the whole energy of the co-ops and the REA was devoted to a struggle for survival. The co-ops, few of which had any surplus funds to pay back to their members, were not concerned with who owned how much of these small businesses. Many members considered that their co-operatives were like municipal systems, owned by the community. But as the co-operatives grew and prospered, members began to ask how they would be credited for the operating surpluses which, except for the heavy loan obligation, normally would be returned to them as patronage refunds. Wickard, who had had a great deal of experience with farm co-ops, was anxious to have this problem solved.

In 1946 the administrator announced that with the help of co-op and legal experts in and out of Government a so-called "Capital Credits Plan" had been worked out. This plan made clear that any payments by farmers for electric service which were in excess of the cost of rendering service belonged and were being credited to the co-op members. At the present time, the plan explained, these excess payments were being used to retire the Government's investment.

Wickard urged the co-ops' directors to adopt this plan, pointing out that it would help show farmers that with each year they owned a greater share of an increasingly valuable property. As payments are made on the government debt, each member would receive a certificate showing his share in the growing equity. These certificates would in turn be retired by new capital furnished by future patronage. The plan of retirement would be in chronological order, the earliest patronage capital being repaid first. Of course the farmer who had made the most use of his co-op's electric service would receive the greater refund, for his contribution to the debt retirement would have been greatest. Wickard has endeavored to make clear to farm co-operators that this is the reason why the farmer's bill is higher than he sometimes thinks it should be. It is also the answer to comparisons sometimes made by the private utilities showing rates somewhat lower than on the co-op lines.

One of the persistent attacks on the co-operatives is on the score of taxation. These attacks ignore, of course, the basic principle of co-operation, which is mutual ownership of an enterprise, with any surplus that may grow out of operation accruing to all member owners in proportion to patronage rather than going as profit to a few owners. Electrical co-op systems pay most forms of state and local taxation that are levied against other businesses.

This issue has become so acute that it even divided the Hoover Commission task force investigating REA along with other government lending agencies. The commission employed a firm of public accountants, Haskins & Sells, to review REA. The task force report, based on the findings of this accounting firm, commented that in

REA accounting no amount was put down as a charge against revenues for federal, state, and local taxes which would have been payable if the REA co-ops were operated by private interests. A minority sharply dissented from the majority report. This minority, consisting of Dean Acheson, James H. Rowe, and James K. Pollock, rebuked the majority for discussing policy rather than confining their critique solely to operation, observing that this was the only Hoover Commission report in which "the commission has abandoned its self-imposed discipline to refrain from comment on the wisdom of statutory enactment." The minority were especially critical of the accounting firm "for adopting the line of private utilities." The statement of the majority was especially pleading, according to the opinion prepared by the minority, and that opinion added, "There can be no loss of something we never had; but there have been great public benefits from the wider availability of electricity on the farm."

Carmody, before Wickard, had faced the tax problem. The co-ops were in some instances assessed taxes based on the physical valuation of their property. REA lawyers and the co-ops argued that co-ops should be taxed according to their ability to pay, rather than in proportion to the book value of their lines. Certainly two railroads, one serving sparsely settled country, the other a dense urban section, would not be assessed at the same value although they had the same physical mileage in line and equipment. Most states have recognized this ability to pay standard, and a few have granted co-ops special tax preference. Inevitably the utility industry has seized upon this to buttress their argument that the co-ops do not pay taxes.

The focal point of the commercial utility's attack is in the matter of income tax. The National Tax Equality Association, which speaks for many large power companies, argues that the net margin between the co-operative's cost of rendering service and the payments by farmer members for electricity should be considered profit. This argument ignores the fact that co-operatives render service at cost; that their rates are set at the lowest point consistent with self-sufficiency. Also ignored is the fact that any net margin is credited to the members, and will be returned to members when the financial condition of the co-op permits. Meanwhile this net margin is being used as new capital replacing old, and as such clearly cannot be considered net profit.

Statistics are only one measure, and perhaps not even the most important yardstick, of REA's achievement. In less than twenty years the co-ops have built more than one million miles of electric power line to serve some three and a half million consumers. An estimated fifty per cent plus of all electrified farms are served by co-operatives; forty-four per cent by the power companies, and the balance by public utility districts and other sources. Of the farms electrified since 1935, about sixty per cent are served by co-ops. This percentage increases progressively so that for the period since Pearl Harbor it is about two thirds, since V-J Day seventy per cent, and since 1949 eighty per cent. Those who look at the record with any objectivity cannot escape the conclusion that nothing like this volume would have been achieved had it not been for the unique partnership of men on the farm working with Government.

No operating co-op has failed, and delinquency on REA loans is less than one half of one per cent. Critics of the program made much of the bookkeeping loss that a quarter of the co-operatives show overlooking the fact this is a temporary situation experienced by almost every new business. In the meantime their cash position is sound, enabling many co-ops to pay back their debt far ahead of schedule.

In 1934 Morris Cooke estimated that at prices then prevailing it would cost about two billion dollars to electrify the three and a half million farms. In the intervening years prices have nearly doubled. Yet power has been brought to that number of farms at a cost fractionally less than Cooke's estimate. That is a measure of REA's efficiency.

IN THE SOUTH more than in any other part of the country the transformation worked by the rural power program is evident. There is a deep-seated consciousness of the benefits it has brought, a proud awareness of the changes that have come over the region. This fact of regional awareness worked in the first instance to get the program going. The long-accumulated sense of injustice coming out of the tragic era in the aftermath of 1865, the struggle to build the "new South," the disparities between the dominant East and the semi-colonial South—all this went into the determination of the South to have whatever was coming. In Washington, as the New Deal got going, southern legislators had this feeling at their backs. They were bound to get as much as any other region and more, too, if they could.

James B. Polhill, Jr., manager of the Jefferson County Electric Membership Corporation, and business manager of the *News and Farmer* of Louisville, Georgia, has been with rural power development from the beginning. He is a big, solid substantial man with an earthy sense of humor. He likes to tell about how he first heard of the REA program. In Atlanta he met someone who said this REA business was about to happen, that they were going to put electricity on the farms. And it was going to be done by the farmers themselves through their own co-operative organizations.

It sounded crazy. Not only crazy but impossible. The fact was that most people on Georgia's farms didn't even want electricity. That was something far beyond their hopes and desires. The farm cycle in Georgia had played itself out. The old plantation families had long ago moved to the towns. They left behind the overseer. When the system of the overseer failed, along came the share cropper, and that was the end of the row. The soil was being mined out, and the people left behind on the soil were mined out too. "Tobacco Road" was a crude literary cliche deeply resented by Georgians—and particularly because it had come from one who had been a Georgian. But the resentment owed something to a kernel of bitter truth behind the stereotype.

Jim Polhill remembers when the first mass meeting was held at the Blundale School in Emanuel County. Some people wanted the electric lines run to their farms, but others wanted no part of this citified idea. And that same thing was true in all of the eleven counties where Polhill and the others were working to get an REA program started. Jim Polhill confesses that he himself had doubts. But then they were throwing all that money around and he figured the Georgia farmers might just as well get some of it. Some farmers signed up for "lights," thinking that the lines would never be built. It all had a vague and uncertain sound.

But when the first lines were built, everything was changed. This was it. You could see what it did. As Polhill has put it, the program spread like a wind-driven fire in a dry broom-sage field. And it has gone on spreading until today nearly all of Georgia's farms have electric power.

Meeting with Polhill, Valene Bennett, Walter Harrison, T. H. Mason, and the others who have had so much to do with making the program a success, you get a sense of what REA has meant in Georgia and throughout all of the South. These men—and they are hard-working, organizing, intensely practical Americans—believe that power on the farms has supplied the margin to work the transformation from Tobacco Road to modern twentieth-century farming. Worn and eroded fields have been brought back with lespedeza and a variety of clovers and other cover crops.

The growing of poultry has developed enormously. In the five years from 1940 to 1945 production went from a million and a half to fifteen million chickens, and the rise was even greater in the following five years. In the eroded hills of North Georgia the growing of ten-week broilers has in large areas replaced the row-crop cotton farming. In Cherokee County in 1930, 23,800 acres of cotton were planted, while in 1950 the total was only 1333 acres.

Guy Stencil had left the farm to earn a kind of living as a barber in the town of Tate. He studied the poultry business and in 1938 went back to the farm. He has since bought and rejuvenated three worn-out farms and he has done it with broilers, and with cattle as a side line. As reported in the *Southeastern Poultryman*, his present farm has eight buildings with a capacity for twenty-six thousand birds without overcrowding. All these buildings are equipped with automatic waterers and some with automatic feeders powered with electricity. He grows four batches a year. In 1950 he marketed more than a hundred thousand broilers. Water is pumped from a spring-fed artificial lake. No cotton is grown on the Stencil farm. And while this may be larger than most farms, there are many like it in Cherokee, Forsyth, and Hall counties.

They talk about this new farm life in the South, especially in Georgia. They paint pictures about it. In the new REA Building in Louisville there is a mural done by Wilmer Wallace of Louisville and Augusta. It is on the wall facing the main entrance so that everyone who comes in to pay his bill, or to talk about getting service, or just to pass the time of day, can see it. It shows the transforming influence of electric power on Georgia's farms. To the left is an unpainted dilapidated farmhouse; in the middle the transition is occurring; and on the right is a farmhouse remodeled, painted, cattle in the pasture, and chickens in the hen house. They even write poems about rural electrification. Walter Paschall, news commentator for the Atlanta Journal, was stopping overnight in Jim Polhill's home and they sat up talking until very late—talking, of course, about what rural power had done. Or, rather, Jim did most of the talking. The next morning Paschall gave Jim the following poem, which was first printed in the Rural Electrification News and from there picked up in newsletters in every state in the country.

> Leave your plow, lad, a moment. Press you ear
> In wonder to this post. You hear the hum?
> It is the song of heartstrings, the faint cry
> of generations.
>
> Over the Georgia hills
> These slender sentinels stand proud, and fling
> Their shining roadway for the kindly slave,
> The many-fingered genii, to come in
> Out of the strength of earth and roaring water
> To blaze against the shadowed ignorance.
>
> (Out of the darkness, light. Out of despair
> The new fulfillment of equality.)
>
> This is your heritage. It came to birth
> From brains of men who strove to lift the curse
> Of useless labor from too-burdened flesh.
> It is democracy at work—the bond
> Of brotherhood between all men who seek
> To raise themselves forever from the beast.
>
> You hear the hum, lad? Ah, then turn away.
> The plow still waits, but you can hold your head
> The higher, knowing that you grasp the hand
> Of all the world upon this throbbing wire.

The relationship between the power company and the REA co-ops is more interesting in Georgia than in perhaps any other state. In fact, in many respects it is a unique relationship. There are several reasons why this should be so, but the chief one is Charles A. Collier, executive vice-president of the Georgia Power Company. Collier is a Georgian first and a power company executive second. At any rate, this is his explanation of why he has worked so closely from the first with REA and the co-operatives.

Collier, who initiated his own statewide improvement plan with a contest among municipalities for the town showing the greatest development in starting new businesses and getting stores and houses painted, talks about the progress in ending Georgia's status as a colonial hewer of wood and drawer of water with the same zeal as the co-operative leaders. One of the resources drawn off from Georgia in the past, according to Collier, was a crop of human beings. Georgia raised them and gave them a primary education, and then they went off to seek work elsewhere because the opportunities simply did not exist at home. Now Collier, says, that trend has for the first time been reversed and the state has begun to gain in population. Families are moving back to the farms and the young people are content to stay there.

The Georgia Power Company under Collier's direction initiated a program of collaboration with REA in the summer of 1936 in an advertisement which received wide circulation in daily and weekly newspapers throughout the state. This advertisement was headlined, "For an electrified Georgia. Where we ourselves can't build, we will help others to build." This was, of course, in striking contrast to the attitude taken at that time by most of the private utilities in the country. The ad pointed out that the company was pressing ahead with building 1026 miles of rural line during 1936 alone to serve 20,000 Georgians in 8000 homes that had never before had electricity. Then the advertisement went on to say:

"The Company cannot build all the lines people want or need—or all the lines we would like to build. We can, however, *help* to get the other lines built and *will* do it. Millions of dollars have been appropriated to the Rural Electrification Administration of the federal Government. This money is to be loaned on easy terms to local associations known as co-operatives, whose members will own and operate the rural electric lines serving their homes and farms. It opens up an opportunity for the electrification of certain sections of Georgia which we frankly admit the Company cannot serve because of its limited funds. This advertisement is published to confirm in fuller detail our previous announcement that the Company will give every public assistance to these co-operatives."

Then the advertisement spelled out the ways in which the power company would help the co-ops get started. It would make preliminary surveys without charge; carry out the maintenance of lines at actual cost; repair and maintain electrical equipment at cost, and perform the job of meter reading and billing also at cost if the co-ops desired. But, most important of all, the advertisement said:

"The Company will supply power at wholesale rates to the co-operatives desiring our service. Rates covering this class of service already have been filed with and accepted by the Georgia Public Service Corporation. They have also been endorsed as reasonable by the REA. These rates are practically identical with the low rates now in effect for the wholesale purchase by municipalities of comparable amounts of power."

In May of 1950, on REA's fifteenth birthday, the company reprinted that original advertisement. In this anniversary advertisement the company said that through the years it had been working side by side with REA co-operatives. While the job of extending service to rural Georgians was ninety per cent completed, according to the ad, that would not signal the end of co-operation between the company and the REA. Georgia Power would continue to supply REA co-operatives "with dependable electric power at low wholesale rates, rates so low that farmers throughout the state can make the fullest use of electricity." Another advertisement later in the same year showed two trucks, one with an REA symbol on it, the other with a Georgia power company symbol. And the caption said, "Two trucks—one errand!" In this second advertisement the company stated that since World War II it had increased its generating capacity by four hundred thousand horse power, or more than half. That much more power was to be added in the next three-year period.

Collier pushed his co-operation with REA a step farther when co-ops in the southern tier of Georgia counties found it difficult to get sufficient power from the Georgia Power and Light Company operating in that area. This company is entirely separate from Georgia Power. As worked out by Collier, a three-way contract was signed. Under that contract Georgia Power delivered power to Georgia Power and Light at a price of 6.5 mills per kilowatt-hour. The smaller company contracted in its turn to sell this to co-operatives at a rate of 7.75 mills and to municipalities at 8.5 mills. When the towns acquire their own transformer substations the price will be reduced to the same level paid by the co-ops. Formerly the co-operatives in these southern counties had been paying 12 and 12.5 mills per kilowatt-hour. The contract signed in 1949 runs for five years, but the co-operative has the right to cancel at the end of three. Hailing this agreement on the floor of the House, Representative John Wheeler of Georgia said:

"The three-way agreement is a fine example of the constructive results which can be achieved by a spirit of mutual helpfulness between private utilities and REA co-operatives. It marks a milestone in electrical progress from which a whole region benefits."

Of the forty-one REA co-ops in Georgia, the Georgia Power Company serves thirty-three, Georgia Power and Light two, the two companies jointly four and TVA two. Revenue to the big power company has steadily increased from $6312 in 1937 to $1,922,858 in 1950. And the average rate per kilowatt-hour has declined in proportion from 1.408 to .674 in 1950. To complete the statistics, the number of consumers connected on all co-ops has gone in the same period from about 8000 to 204,000, and the number of miles energized from 3000 to 53,621.

In Collier's files are a series of letters from co-ops throughout Georgia expressing appreciation for services the company has provided from time to time over the years. These letters show particular enthusiasm for the home economics instruction and guidance provided to REA specialists by the company. This file of letters should be instructive reading for other utility executives who have carried on incessant war with the REA co-operatives.

The Georgia Power Company is a very prosperous concern and no one would be likely to accuse Collier of being a starry-eyed idealist. Yet many of his fellow utility executives from other parts of the country look at him askance. In several instances he has withdrawn the support of his company from participation in advertising programs attacking the REA. The explanation may be simply that he is a Georgian with a deep sense of dedication to the progress and development of his state, that he possesses a determination to build it up to the level of the North. It may be shrewd business sense. After all, not a single co-operative in Georgia generates its own power.

The skeptical on the other side of the power argument point to this fact to underscore their suspicion that the policy of the company is part of a carefully planned strategy. Because there is no generation, the co-ops are entirely dependent on the Georgia Power Company. Furthermore, Congress cut out the Department of Interior appropriation to link private and public power units in order to step up the whole supply for the state. Writing in *Rural Georgia*, the official publication of the statewide co-op association, Walter Harrison, the editor, said:

"It was proposed that from this fund 'backbone' transmission lines would be developed in Georgia. . . . By this construction it would have meant tying in with the utility interests of this state and would have made available to them certain energy that was not needed by public bodies, such as REA, municipalities, and federal installations. These lines would have meant that the people whose taxes are financing these ventures would get the full benefit from these projects, as was the intention of Congress when the act was drawn in 1944. If these lines are not built and unless unusual contracts are drawn, the utility interests of this section will benefit the most and at the expense of the taxpayers."

Harrison, who typifies the able and alert leadership at the top of the Georgia program, has close ties with the state's influential delegation in Congress. It is likely that in the future the pressures on this delegation will increase to support appropriations to strengthen and expand the power grid on which the co-ops depend. There are greater potentialities for all concerned in the big hydro projects completed or nearing completion in the rivers of the Southeast that are now being realized.

In the South, as everywhere else, the variations among co-operatives are great. Pickens, South Carolina, is set in the Piedmont section of the state where the foothills of the Blue Ridge start to steepen sharply. It is in the last chain of the towns that have attracted industry because of climate, cheap power, and "good labor relations." The pattern of the past is swiftly changing. The full-time farmer is disappearing. Now many men work in the mills and do part-time farming when they are not on shift, and over the week ends.

The Pickens rural area is about eighty-five per cent electrified. The Blue Ridge Co-operative is doing a good job in the extension of lines through the mountainous country. Even the modest weather-beaten cabins up in the hills are reached by the co-op. Some of these one-room cabins are so small that their refrigerators and washing machines overflow onto the open porches. Despite the achievements of the Blue Ridge co-op, the passing visitor feels that something is lacking.

The annual meeting of the Blue Ridge Co-operative is poorly attended. Only about twenty-five people turn out from a membership of four thousand farmers. The manager, Jud Hurt, a young engineer with a personable air, is somewhat embarrassed by this meager showing. He and the directors put the poor attendance down to the spring rains which left the farmers so far behind in their plowing that they did not want to lose a single good day. They also explained that many of the members are not really farmers but industrial workers who do part-time farming and who have, therefore, only a light allegiance to what is in essence a farm organization. Jud Hurt repeats what a preacher in the mountains told him, "Don't worry, son; if they don't come, it's because they are satisfied. If the members thought there was anything wrong, you would have eight thousand of 'em in town." And Hurt himself attributes the small attendance to satisfaction with the management.

This may be true, but the observer senses a lack of the kind of understanding that means integration within the community. Perhaps the overworked expression "public relations" covers it. The co-op has no home economist. The agricultural engineer is a lad just out of Clemson College who has been preoccupied with his troubles with the draft. What is lacking may well be more important than anything that could be provided in the guise of "public relations" as that term is ordinarily understood.

In South Carolina rural electrification was first set up under a state administration on the theory that in this way overhead could be cut down. Central engineering services and central auditing could be provided and overlapping construction could be eliminated. John Carmody, second REA administrator, had warned of the apathy that would develop in such an arrangement, and he struggled hard to prevent any middlemen from coming in between the Rural Electrification Administration and the individual co-operatives.

In 1940 the state program was split into twenty-three districts with a co-operative created for each of the districts. In this way it was thought that a greater interest would be stimulated, with co-operators developing a sense of ownership and responsibility. But without the most carefully directed public relations, the sense of co-operation and achievement that elsewhere grew out of the often fierce struggle of farmers to get electricity could not be generated.

In the town of Pickens, the Blue Ridge co-op is pretty much taken for granted. The banker, the Chevrolet dealer, the men who own the drugstore and the hardware store, as well as the hotelkeeper, are inclined to say, well, yes, it's a pretty good thing. Even the Rotary is resigned to the existence of this $2,500,000 business.

The Duke Power Company, the co-op's wholesale supplier, seems fairly friendly. At one time the company reported to the Blue Ridge directors that it would not be able to supply all the power the co-op wanted, since there was a shortage of generating capacity. When the Blue Ridge co-op applied to REA for a generating-plant loan, the company wrote a letter saying that it would supply all the power needed. The power companies never change, says Hurt.

The Southside Electric Co-operative at Crewe, Virginia, provides a marked contrast. Here there is a carefully planned effort to build a sense of mutual responsibility and at the same time increase the use of electric power as widely as possible. Four thousand farmers came to Southside's annual meeting in 1951. Such attendance is indicative of the role this co-op plays in the lives of its nine thousand members. Located southwest of Richmond, the countryside shows its early origin by county names such as Sussex, Isle of Wight, and Prince Edward. Tobacco has for a very long time been the principal crop, but electricity is making possible the beginning of more diversified agriculture. Dairying and truck farming are replacing the old cash crop, tobacco. Through this diversified agriculture, farmers are finding new security and a higher standard of living.

The Southside co-op is big business. But by its very size the five-million-dollar company, touching fourteen Virginia counties, is faced with problems of remoteness from the consumer-owner that the co-operative tries to bridge through a series of district meetings. These district meetings precede the large annual meeting in the Crewe ball park. Held at night in a local schoolhouse or grange, these meetings help the co-op management keep in touch with the members and their individual problems.

One such meeting held at the Bellefont Grange is typical. Besides the staff of the co-op, about seventy-five co-op members are gathered in the Grange's cement block building. There are door prizes—a bridge lamp, a table lamp, and a utility lamp—provided by local appliance dealers. These dealers are always glad to donate the prizes, according to the Southside manager Charles Hooper, in gratitude for the great volume of business REA has brought to the community. Each of three dealers has, since 1937, according to Hooper, sold about a quarter of a million dollars' worth of appliances to Southside members.

The chief feature of the evening is the showing of a movie in color of the work of the co-operative. Made by a public-relations firm in Richmond, it shows the ultramodern administration building at Crewe, the electrical substations, the radio communications system between the administration building and the co-op's fourteen trucks, the visit of the co-op's home economist to a member's home, and the different uses that electricity can be put to in the barns and elsewhere. The film also shows how electricity has made possible the rise of small rural industries such as sawmills, chicken hatcheries, and service stations that formerly were confined to towns where electric power was available. Showing the first beginnings of the co-op in 1937 when three hundred members were hooked up, the film underscores the way in which the use of electricity has grown sixfold, from 41 to 250 kilowatt-hours a month.

After the showing Manager Hooper tells the audience that it is now the members' turn to present their problems and to ask questions. A young farmer asks about the possibility of getting some of the low-cost power from the federal hydroelectric project on the Roanoke River at Buggs Island. Hooper explains that the Buggs Island Dam will generate 90,000 kilowatts of electricity at first and when completed will generate a total of 200,000 kilowatts. But he also explains how, thanks in large part to the extreme conservatism of the political machine that dominates Virginia, the co-ops will probably be unable to obtain this power except over the lines of a private company which will be able to "fix" the wheeling or carrying charge to be paid by the co-operatives.

Hooper goes on to say that the Southside and other Virginia co-ops had applied to REA in Washington for a 16,000,000 dollar loan so that jointly they might build a transmission line to connect with the federal project. The application was approved by REA, but the Virginia Corporation Commission turned down the federated co-op's construction permit, since the Virginia Electric Power Company had declared that they would wheel the power at "a very cheap rate"—one mill per kilowatt hour. However, when Southside and other co-ops came to sign an agreement with the power company, the price asked was one mill for each fifty miles a kilowatt was wheeled. This meant that the Southside co-op would have to pay a carrying charge of three mills for each kilowatt-hour over and beyond the cost of the power, with the result that the co-op would not benefit from Buggs Island low-cost power.

After several other questions about power supplies and the new telephone program, an elderly lady asks Hooper what she and other members can do to improve their co-operative. Each member of Southside's staff gives his or her answer. The assistant manager, "Please notify us when your power goes off and help us prevent the rifle shooting of the heavy porcelain insulators." The home economist, "Ask more questions. Ask for kitchen demonstrations and for operating directions for home freezers. And please put your names on your mailboxes so I can find you when I come to visit." The office manager, "Please compute and pay your bills promptly." The engineer, "Give us plenty of notice when you want your tenant houses hooked up, as we have a three months' waiting list now. And tell us about rotting poles and slack guy wires." Refrigeration expert, "Give us a chance to teach you the best freezing techniques so you won't lose your produce."

Touring the district, the visitor is aware of how much Hooper, a former vice-president of NRECA, has contributed. He is a capable executive of a business employing eighty-five people working in fourteen counties. He directs this business from a two-story yellow brick building constructed in 1940. His own office is spacious and handsomely furnished, equipped with a dictating machine and intercom system and a large board of directors' table at which he holds the many meetings that take place from week to week.

Hooper has an interesting perspective on the relationship between the private utilities and the co-ops. The main reason the utilities failed to move into rural markets, in his view, was that they made a serious miscalculation about the economic position of the farmer. They looked at figures showing that the average farm income was only $600 to $1000 a year and therefore they concluded that the farmer was unable to afford electricity. What they did not realize was that this was net cash income and that in addition the farmer provided for his own use meat, vegetables, and so forth. This gave him a great advantage over the city man per dollar of income, particularly with the advent of high personal income taxes. And now with electrical equipment he is able to go even further with the storage and preservation of his own food supply.

This able and efficient manager is also interesting on the subject of the limitations in the way of a greatly increased use of electricity. Refrigerators, irons, radios, and television sets can be readily installed. But water pump and inside plumbing often require plumbers who are confined in an ancient craft union, narrowly restricted as to size, and who are, more often than not, content with ancient methods and with the volume of work they can obtain in the towns. They see no point in going far out in the country to work. Furthermore, it is virtually impossible for a nonunion plumber to start in, because the supply houses simply will not sell him supplies. The consequence is high prices that work against the installation of plumbing systems. A recent survey showed that only a third of the members of the Southside co-op had running water in their houses, whereas nearly all had irons and radios and three-quarters had refrigerators.

There is some resistance on the part of the older generation to running water in the house. For this reason, the co-operative is concentrating its educational program on children in the schools. The power of education by example was clearly illustrated during the war years. When soldiers returned home, they and their parents beseiged the co-op with 8500 applications for service. Having seen how people live in the towns and the cities, they were no longer content to go back to the pre-power era. Thanks in part at least to the work of the co-op staff, it can be shown that most members have continued steadily from year to year to use more and more electricity. For instance, nine billings for the first year showed an average monthly use of 77 kilowatt-hours; twelve years later these same billings showed an average of 535 hours.

Another profound change that can be attributed in part at least to the coming of power to the country is the first major construction of farmhouses in more than twenty years. All around, too, you see houses being remodeled. This often follows shortly after the house has been wired for electricity. First the farmer buys some electric appliances. Then he may decide that he needs plumbing. Finding that the shining white stove or refrigerator looks out of place in his old-fashioned kitchen, he goes on to extensive rebuilding.

One such farmer is Walter Arnold. Arnold is a Yankee, having come to Virginia from Rhode Island during the early war years. The Arnold family owned a dairy near Providence whose glass-enclosed milking parlor used to draw admiring crowds on the week ends. Hard times came, and the Arnolds decided to pull up stakes and start over again in Virginia.

Arnold today has a fine dairy farm near Crewe. Natives around there tell you that Walter "dug his farm out of the dirt." There were many hard years when Arnold didn't know whether he would make it or not. He started a dairy herd that today numbers eighty-five cows, and he has now built his own cow barn equipped with electric milking machines, milk coolers, and electric separators. "I couldn't hope to run this place without that electric machinery," says Arnold, "nor could I produce Grade-A milk without the milk cooler. Since Grade-A milk sells for six dollars a hundred pounds and Grade B sells for three dollars, you can see what that cooler means to a dairyman."

In spite of the big job in the dairy, Arnold has found time to remodel his farmhouse, which was built in the early 1700s. This New Englander has restored the pine wainscoting; he has repaired and brought back the wide board floors to their original beauty. But he has done much more than restore the beauty of this farmhouse. He has also installed a modern electric kitchen. An electric range, hot-water heater, refrigerator, and many smaller appliances have relieved the drudgery for Mrs. Arnold. "Of course," Mrs. Arnold says, "I just couldn't stand to get rid of my old wood stove. I wouldn't cook on it any more, but it's useful to warm the kitchen with on cold mornings."

Walter Arnold shows off the electric blower house heater that warms the house through large grates in the floors. "This isn't as good as radiators," he says, "but it certainly is a good deal cheaper."

Above all, one can see in this area where farming in a particular pattern has been carried on for so long, that, the farm home having been transformed through the magic of low-cost power, the pull is now back to the country, where there are advantages that the city and the town do not afford. This means in many instances part-time farming. It means greater stability. It means the beginnings of a trend away from urbanism that has increasingly tended to divorce man from the source of his basic needs and to make him ever more dependent on the kind of huge and complicated organization in which he can have no sense whatsoever of any personal destiny. It was this urbanism that Thomas Jefferson dreaded, and while those who claim to be his heirs and assigns in his native Virginia today raise a loud clamor against anything remotely resembling government participation, including REA, they choose to ignore or deliberately distort the significance of an achievement that is in the spirit if not in the letter of what Jefferson taught when he warned against the threat of an urban growth that would result in dispossessed and rootless masses with no ties to the society in which they happened to live.

For prosperity and seeming contentment, for the integration of the new with the old, it would be hard to find a more conspicuous example than the peninsula on the Eastern Seaboard that is made up of part of Delaware, Maryland, and Virginia. The loamy, sandy soil produces an abundance of fruits and vegetables, crops that are processed in small canning plants throughout the region. Dairy herds supply a share of the vast stream of milk flowing into the great cities of the East. It is the center, too, of a thriving chicken industry—the ten-week broilers produced on virtually an assembly-line basis in great long chicken houses on farm after farm.

Besides this agricultural wealth, a system of rivers and inlets, Chesapeake Bay and the Atlantic Ocean furnish all manner of seafood to augment both the diet and the income of many a farmer in that singularly blessed part of the world. At the heart of this region is the Eastern Shore of Maryland. Here are small towns with village squares surrounded by ancient brick buildings little changed by the passage of a century or a century and a half. The farms are passed on from generation to generation, and your social status in the community tends to turn on how long your family has tilled the same soil. Through this fertile country flows the Choptank River, Choptank being an Indian name meaning crooked river.

The Choptank Electric Co-operative was organized thirteen years ago, with its main office in Denton, Maryland. The Eastern Shore was then only beginning to recover from the long depression. The series of farm bills that were part of the New Deal, calling for parity payments and other forms of assistance to depressed agriculture, had begun to produce at least the beginnings of an upturn.

The towns of the regions were served by the Eastern Shore Public Service Company. This old and conservative operating company had been victimized not by one but by two utility pirates. First was Samuel Insull, who built a fantastic pyramid and when it tottered to ruin fled to Greece, where he hoped extradition would not be able to catch up with him. The second big-time juggler to get control of the Eastern Shore Company was an even more fantastic character, Howard Hopson, who likewise went down to ignominious disaster after his hodgepodge of a utility empire fell to pieces. The depredations of Insull and Hopson made it less likely that the Eastern Shore would be interested in extending its power lines out into the country where, even in such a rich area, the prospect of profit from farm users seemed remote.

The leading farmers in the community around Denton soon were aware of what REA might mean to them. One was Harry H. Nuttle, a director of the Southern States Co-operative. He is also the leading businessman of Denton, owning a lumber mill and supply plant, a canning factory, and a seed business. Nuttle was the moving spirit in getting a group of farmers together to form the Choptank Electric Co-operative. The Choptank co-op's first loan from the REA was for $30,000. Today it has more than 11,000 consumers served by 2700 miles of power line.

From the beginning the relationship of the co-operative and the Eastern Shore Company has been at least comparatively friendly. Under the first contract, power was purchased at wholesale from the company at 13.5 mills a kilowatt-hour, a rate which made it possible to serve rural users of the co-operative lines at a retail rate only slightly above that paid by householders in towns getting their power direct from the private utility. It should be noted, however, that at the last annual meeting of Choptank, the membership approved an item of $10,000 for the purchase of a site for a generating plant. This indicates that there is at least consideration being given to the possibility that relations may not always be so favorable, with the co-op compelled to build its own steam-generating plant.

The Choptank Co-operative got its manager from the Eastern

Shore Company. F. E. Yeoman, an accountant when he moved over, takes an almost paternal pride in the growth of the organization. Standing before the big charts in the co-op's office building completed in 1949, he shows how the rural power lines crisscross in and out through the whole area of the Eastern shore. He demonstrates the two-way radio hookup with each of the co-op's thirteen automobiles and service trucks.

It is not surprising that Choptank has flourished in this prosperous community. But it was not always so prosperous, nor was there always the push-button assistance of electricity. Harry Nuttle was asked to pay nearly six thousand dollars to get the company to string wires to his farm. A rich man, he nevertheless felt that the cost was out of line. It was one of the reasons he was willing to put so much time and energy into the formation of Choptank, of which he has always been a director.

The concept of co-operative distribution enters very little into the scheme of things in this conservative part of the world. Yet sometimes at Rotary meetings Yeoman finds himself in the midst of a sharp argument. "Socialism," some of the more stalwart members will say accusingly. And then he is ready to deny it and to defend what he believes to be the justified place of the co-operative on the Eastern Shore. "But don't you see," he says, "that we aren't the Government, and we aren't getting anything from the Government? We're paying back the loan they let us have and we're paying it back with interest. What's more, if you'll look into it, you'll find that we're not only repaying the loan with interest, but that the Government's net gain on our project is paying most of the cost of administering the REA program. They can do that because they get a higher interest rate from us than they pay people who hold most of the government debt. Now, you can call that socialism. . ."

Sometimes the weekly newspaper in Denton has editorials attacking public power, TVA, and REA as socialistic ventures of the New Deal. Once when Yeoman took the editor to task for such an editorial, he seemed mildly surprised. Was that in the paper? he asked. There are many syndicates that supply filler material for weekly newspapers by the yard, and this includes editorials that take an extreme conservative or reactionary position.

Referring to anything that goes on in this rich conservative community as socialistic seems slightly absurd. From all over the Eastern Shore—Choptank is one of the nation's thirty-three largest co-operatives—the members come for the annual meeting in bright, shiny new cars. For several issues the Choptank *Live Wire* has been building up the importance of this meeting for the effective direction of the organization and also holding out the lure of attractive door prizes. About a thousand members gather in the Dentonia Theater, many of them with their wives and children. The Hurlock

High School Band plays. Then there is square dancing and singing until finally the meeting is called to order at one-thirty by President Harry A. Moore.

It is not precisely a spirited meeting. These people seem well satisfied to leave affairs in the hands of the directors and Manager Yeoman. The nominating committee's slate of seven directors, six of them already serving, is accepted unanimously without a single nomination from the floor. In fact, no one has anything to say from the floor.

The guest speaker is Clyde Ellis of NRECA. He touches upon the familiar theme of the importance of co-operatives and of the threat from the utilities that are anxious to put them out of business. It is a speech meant to rouse this audience of prosperous farm co-operators to the urgent need for low-cost power obtained through their own efforts.

The changes that are coming so fast to the South must be credited in part to the extraordinary experiment that has taken place since 1933 in the Tennessee Valley. Here grew the origins of much of the rural electrification program. In 1934 Morris Cooke studied the operations of the Alcorn County Co-operative at Corinth, Mississippi, to determine what role the co-operative should play in the national rural power program. The "yardstick" rates of the TVA helped to prove that low-cost power meant high usage. The experiments with electric power in farm production in the TVA region have been copied in all parts of the country.

But it should be added that the TVA's rural power program also has been vitalized by the REA program. The concept of area coverage, which led to ultimate system planning, was not fully appreciated in the TVA area until as late as 1945. Only the more densely populated rural areas were served, leaving Tennessee behind other states in the region, such as Georgia, North Carolina, Alabama, and Virginia. Of course there were reasons other than area coverage that caused Tennessee to lag behind, one of them being the wartime demands on TVA for industrial power.

One of the leaders of rural electrification in the TVA area is Knox Hutchinson. An educator for the greater part of his life, Hutchinson began to help organize electric co-ops in 1935, eventually becoming president of the Middle Tennessee Electric Membership Corporation, and the Statewide Co-operative Association.

"Doc", as Hutchinson is known, is a handsome man in his late fifties. Having taught at several agricultural schools, he is practicing what he preaches. His 850-acre farm near Murfreesboro, Tennessee, is a model for the intelligent application of electricity to farm production. His farming is diversified—he has orchards, grain, poultry, and some sheep—all carefully planned. For his farm work he was named "The Man of the Year in Tennessee Agriculture" by the *Progressive Farmer Magazine.*

Hutchinson was appointed Assistant Secretary of Agriculture in 1949. Here he is in a position to survey the whole of American farming. He says he knows of nothing that has influenced American farm life in its entirety the way electricity has. Not only has farm production been affected, but so has the whole outlook of rural people. "They are becoming better citizens," Hutchinson says, "citizens with an increasing interest in local and national affairs. And remember this: rural electrification is just reaching the commencement period. Up until now we have just been getting together the physical things, such as poles and lines. The full use of electricity in the farm life of the South and the nation remains for tomorrow."

IN WISCONSIN where so much social and economic legislation has been pioneered the rural electric co-operatives have taken the lead in advances that have had an influence not only throughout the Midwest but the nation. The first statewide co-operative was formed in Wisconsin at a time when the policy of the REA in Washington was opposed to statewide organizations. The Wisconsin Electric Co-operative, as it was eventually called, published the first statewide paper, the *Wisconsin REA News*.

Before the statewide organization was formed in 1936, the then Governor, Philip La Follette, had appointed a Rural Electrification Co-ordination Committee to help groups of farmers organize and prepare applications for REA loans. La Follette followed this up by forming the Wisconsin Development Authority, a state agency to provide services, and particularly engineering service, to these same groups.

But after the defeat of La Follette's Progressive administration in 1938, the farmers began to learn that they were on their own. They could no longer count on the state for the support they needed. That was when certain co-op leaders realized that they could not look to government to perform services which should necessarily be carried out through their own organization.

Short of a separate book, it is impossible to do more than summarize the accomplishments of the Wisconsin Electric Co-operative. From the beginning it has been an aggressive organization, seeking to make the fullest use of the political power of the farm families who had come together to obtain electric service for themselves.

While the private utilities, following the initiation of the REA program, reduced their rural rates and accelerated the construction of lines into the country, they also began to build spite lines intended to skim off the cream of the farm business. Through the focus of WEC, co-operators were able to get legislation passed restricting this practice. The organization also helped to bring about adoption of a tax system based on the ability of the co-ops to pay. Numerous attempts to handicap co-operative development through discriminatory controls and unfair taxes were rebuffed by the vigilance of the statewide.

WEC set out originally to provide engineering service for member co-operatives. This function was later delegated to the Wisconsin Development Authority. At that time the statewide's staff was reduced to one clerk in the mistaken belief that, with the pioneering stage past, its role was about ended. But that clerk was William V.

Thomas, who was later to become general manager. Bill Thomas decided that the organization could prove its usefulness by helping member co-ops obtain material at a lower cost.

He initiated a program for the purchase of line supplies which began on a modest scale and almost immediately encountered opposition from the National Electrical Manufacturers Association. The association set out to get all their members to cancel contracts with WEC. But Wisconsin has a law forbidding any discrimination against co-operatives and the manufacturers were charged with violating this law. The charge was sustained and WEC has ever since continued to expand its supply service.

Today the line materials department helps to furnish member co-ops not only in Wisconsin but in North and South Dakota, Nebraska, Minnesota, Illinois, Iowa, Missouri, Kansas, and Oklahoma with construction materials on a co-operative basis. Field representatives for WEC call on the individual co-ops in those states to help them solve their problems. Branch offices and warehouses are maintained in Moorhead, Minnesota, and Kansas City, Missouri.

Perhaps the most dramatic achievement of WEC was its part in breaking the bottleneck in aluminum cable in 1948. As was told in an earlier chapter, officials of the National Rural Electric Co-operative Association had reached an agreement with the Reynolds Metals Company to produce the necessary cable. But an experienced agent was still needed to enter a contract with the Reynolds Company. NRECA turned to the Wisconsin Electric Co-operative as the only organization that could conceivably do the job.

As Norris Maloney, attorney for WEC, pointed out in a speech at the dedication of a new headquarters building at Madison in August of 1951, this was a tough decision, for it meant risking the whole future of what had been up to that point a highly successful co-operative venture. But WEC's distribution of aluminum cable to REA co-ops on a nationwide basis proved successful. The bottleneck was broken as the other aluminum companies suddenly discovered that they could give delivery on ten days' or two weeks' notice.

WEC has long since restored its engineering service, which had been widely used. Member co-ops are not assessed a membership fee for carrying on the activities of the statewide organization. They pay for individual services and the revenue has been more than adequate to absorb all costs and in addition to provide substantial dividends to members.

In still another field Wisconsin co-operatives have pioneered. They have formed the Dairyland Power Co-operative, the largest generating and transmission co-op, with $25,000,000 invested in plants and another $10,000,000 in lines. It serves nearly 80,000 farmers, who belong to the twenty-five distribution co-operatives that are members of the federation owning Dairyland. These farmers are the backbone of the rich dairy industry in Wisconsin, Minnesota, Illinois, and Iowa. By 1951 Dairyland was preparing to provide energy to nearly a hundred thousand users each using on the average in excess of 550 kw-h per month.

Among the men who initiated and carried through this great cooperative venture were followers of "Fighting Bob" La Follette, who had long believed in the co-operative idea. The co-operative concept, originating in Norway, Sweden, and Finland, was given a new and vigorous direction within the framework of the La Follette Progressive movement. Such men as William E. Rabe, H .O. Melby, and Wallace Landry devoted literally months and months of their time to an undertaking that developed out of the need of farmer members for low-cost power. They worked to master the intricacies of a complex venture instead of relying on paid experts. In this same category was George A. Lewis, who helped in the first instance to form the Rural Electrification Co-ordination Committee under Governor Phil La Follette. Lewis then represented the Farmers' Union.

Many of the pioneers are still carrying the heaviest part of the burden as officers of Dairyland, giving their time freely and uncomplainingly. For them, and for many others who were part of the common cause, a ceremony held on a hot July day in 1951 at Cassville, Wisconsin, was a stirring kind of climax, a day to stop and look with pride and pleasure at what had been done. This was the dedication of the E. J. Stoneman Steam Power Plant.

"E.J." was one of those who had worked to create Dairyland. One of the founders of NRECA, he was its first vice-president and its second president. Although he had come out of schoolteaching to co-operation and had come comparatively late to the co-operative idea, he had worked with such zeal and energy he undoubtedly shortened his life. Here were his widow, his daughters and son, his friends who had stood side by side with him in the long and patient struggle.

The big power plant was decked with flags and bunting and in a tent nearby the women of Cassville served lunch cafeteria-style. In the auditorium-like generating room, where still another unit is eventually to be installed, a speaker's stand was set up. One after the other the speakers paid tribute to the man who had contributed so much to making this possible.

One speaker was John E. Olson, who had succeeded Stoneman as president of Dairyland. Olson has the solid look of the Scandinavians who have helped to make Wisconsin a great state. He spoke with slow, quiet dignity of the work they had shared, "E.J." and all the others, reaching back into each community to create Dairyland.

The plant is a thing of steel, of brick and mortar, of great machines. But, listening, one could not help feeling with these men who had struggled and worked for it that it is a great deal more than that. It is something into which they have put their own hopes and beliefs, their own patient and persistent efforts. It was not done on order from Washington or New York. When, for purposes of the ceremony, steam was released into the boiler and the whirring sound of the turbines began again, it was a moment solemn and moving and yet with a sense of reward and achievement.

Dairyland had a four-seater plane used by the management and the directors to get about from one to the other of the eleven generating stations. It was late afternoon when we left Cassville and flew up the Mississippi over the steam plant at Genoa, stopping briefly to refuel at La Crosse, then on to Alma, which is the largest co-operatively owned steam-generating plant in the world. We left the Mississippi and flew north over increasingly wooded country, circling over Dairyland's big hydro plant on the Flambeau River at Ladysmith.

There in the clear sun of late afternoon was the broad newly created lake, its shores looking as untouched as though this were virgin territory. The great earth dyke was linked by a solid mass of concrete like a bridge in the center, and all of it seeming, on this still afternoon, to have been put down in the wooded countryside by some magic without any human intervention. But into it had gone time, toil, patience. After all, it had cost $6,000,000, and the lake-reservoir covers two thousand acres with a sixty-five foot edge of water behind the dam.

The origin of Dairyland can be traced back to 1937 when representatives of ten electric distribution co-operatives met to discuss a common problem—how to obtain adequate wholesale power at reasonable rates. The co-ops had all been organized within a year after the passage of the REA Act. And all of them had engaged in long drawn-out negotiations with wholesale power producers. The ten represented at that meeting were Buffalo, Chippewa Valley, Clark, Dunn, Pierce-Pepin, Taylor, Trempealeau, Jackson, St. Croix, and Eau Claire. They felt the offers they had had from power companies—starting at 2½ cents per kw-h—were too high and they were determined to investigate the feasibility of building their own plant.

The new federation formed by the ten co-ops applied to REA for a loan of $650,000, which was approved in April of 1937. REA's rate experts estimated in that early stage that the plant would save members at least $30,000 a year over the best long-term contract for power that had been offered by the utilities. A 2100-kw Diesel generating plant was built at Chippewa Falls and was in operation the following spring. It began to serve seven of the distribution co-ops on 243 miles of transmission line. The other three—Jackson, St. Croix, and Eau Claire—were scheduled for service as soon as their first lines were energized.

In the southern part of the state other distribution co-operatives were having the same sort of difficulty. There, too, they were unable to negotiate contracts for power at a reasonable rate. Co-operative leaders from Grant, Crawford, Richland, Lafayette, and Vernon counties met at Boscobel in December of 1938 to talk about building their own generating facilities. In neighboring Iowa and Minnesota co-ops faced the same problem and their representatives were invited to that first meeting. Out of it came the Tri-State Power Co-operative. Many of the leaders in the southern group still did not expect to begin actual construction. They believed that the very organization of a generating co-op would be a bargaining lever sufficient to persuade companies in the area to lower rates. But it did not work that way.

In March of 1939 the directors of Tri-State realized that they would have to proceed with plans for construction. Ironically enough, after thousands of dollars had been spent and plans were nearing completion for the erection of a modern steam-generating plant at Genoa, the co-operatives received a new offer from three utilities serving the area. The rate was not unattractive. Had it been presented before the expenditure of funds in organization and planning, the offer would undoubtedly have been accepted and the Tri-State Power Co-op would never have functioned. The first energy flowed from the Genoa plant in May of 1941.

For some time thought had been given to the possibility of interconnecting the southern and northern system for interchange of power and economy of operation. Merger of the two in the Dairyland Power Co-operative did not occur until October of that same year. The consolidation was recommended by REA because the Wisconsin Power co-op had found that already the load demand was taxing its capacity even though the Chippewa plant had been doubled to 4200 kw. Tri-State, with a generating capacity of 8000 kw at Genoa, had power to supply its members and at the same time to handle a portion of the northern co-operative's load. Then, too, the combined organization would have stand-by power available in case one plant in the system had a power failure. At the outset Dairyland was composed of twenty-three distribution co-ops serving more than 25,000 members.

The war stopped further expansion. One steam unit was actually about to be installed as an addition to the plant at Genoa when it was requisitioned by the Navy. According to rumor, it remained crated up on a dock in Puerto Rico throughout the war. As the demand for electricity among the members mounted, Dairyland was compelled to turn to commercial power suppliers. Not until 1945 did the situation ease sufficiently so the co-op could install two 4000-kw units at Genoa.

Growth came rapidly after this. Membership doubled and then tripled as the distribution co-ops pushed ahead toward area coverage. The new steam plant at Alma, completed in September of 1947, contained two units capable of producing as much power as the three previously built plants combined. A third unit added last year makes Alma the largest co-operatively owned generating plant in the world.

All this had not been accomplished without strong opposition from the industry. That opposition finally was concentrated on blocking the hydro plant to be built on the Flambeau River. The first application was filed by Dairyland with the Wisconsin Public Service Commission in November, 1946. This marked the beginning of a long and bitter struggle. The first public hearing was held at Ladysmith the following January.

Loyal co-op members packed the hearing room and waited outside to take their turn to testify. They followed closely every word spoken in the crowded room. From Ladysmith the scene of the struggle shifted to the state legislature in Madison. Here again farmer members turned out in impressive numbers to let their representatives know that this was something they meant to have. The Public Service Commission considered the petition almost two years and through 1493 pages of testimony and 102 exhibits. High-priced lawyers by the score presented the opposition case for the power companies. Nor did the opponents neglect to bring influence on REA in Washington, where Dairyland's application for a loan was pending.

But the Public Service Commission was not entirely responsible for the delay. Ernest Swift, assistant director of the State Conservation Department, asked that consideration of the project be postponed, claiming that his department had no knowledge of the proposed dam before the hearing, despite the fact that the co-op's petition had been filed several months before. Conservationists of the extremist type were anxious to express their views on how the dam and reservoir would destroy the natural beauty of the site.

This opposition and the resulting delays were a serious matter for Dairyland. Besides the great need for the power potential, a prolonged postponement might undermine all the careful planning of costs of construction and operation. Engineers had testified that the dam, which would cost $3,000,000 and have a rated capacity of 15,000 kilowatts, could generate power for less than four mills per kilowatt-hour and be amortized within the loan period at that rate. This rate was less than half the cost of generation at any of Dairyland's other plants. But this was a period of rapidly rising costs and the inflationary spiral threatened to push the cost of construction far above the estimates.

The conservation argument had to be met head-on. Dairyland lawyers and researchers came up with the fact, carefully documented, that never more than fifty canoe parties in any one season had ever in recent years used the river. The cost of each canoe trip, on the basis of hydro power and the cost of steam power at Alma, was estimated at $4061 for a trip lasting two to three hours.

"We think conservation of human resources is the most important kind of conservation, and our farm families need this power for better and more productive living," Rabe testified.

On October 15, 1947, power company and co-op executives agreed to end the controversy with the company leasing its three dams to Dairyland and withdrawing its opposition. This was on condition that REA and the Public Service Commission approve the agreement. A contract was signed in January of the following year which was later approved by Administrator Wickard. On August 2, twenty-one months after the application was filed, the commission approved the project. In spite of orders to the contrary by the Conservation Commission, the Conservation Department continued to oppose the project.

The tragic cost of all this was revealed when bids were opened in September. They were approximately double the engineering estimates of two years before. New bids were called for and these proved to be somewhat more reasonable. But nevertheless it was necessary to get a supplementary loan of $2,770,000 to cover the incease in costs since the original loan of $3,730,000 had been approved in 1946.

The cost of this deliberate obstructionism has been put at roughly a million dollars. This is the amount by which prices increased as a result of needless delays. Naturally this is reflected in the monthly power bill. Dairyland's operating costs at Flambeau are about five mills per kilowatt-hour, which is still less than the cost of production at any plant in the system.

Construction was begun in 1949. Just under two years later, the Flambeau plant came into operation and added 17,000 kw to the system. The generating capacity of the entire system is now 127,000 kw. In the last annual statement Manager John P. Madgett reported that, in 1950, 128 miles of transmission line and sixteen substations had been added. The transmission line figure does not include the largest project of all, the 71-mile 138-kv transmission line which provides a heavy tie between the Alma and Genoa stations.

Planning for at least ten years in advance is going forward. The annual reports bristle with statistics. They are statistics of which co-op members are enormously proud. They are proudest of all of the figures showing that Dairyland saved its members more than $2,000,000 in 1950 alone over the best power rates offered by utilities when the distributing co-ops in their beginning phase were trying to get reasonable wholesale rates.

Administrator Wickard came from Washington to speak at the

dedication of the Stoneman plant, which eventually will be the largest of the eleven in the Dairyland system. A unit is under construction that will double the plant's present capacity some time in 1952 if present construction schedules are not interrupted. In his speech Wickard said:

"Farmers have to rely upon their power supplier to obtain adequate sources of power and see that this power is delivered to their farms in a reliable and satisfactory manner. They, unlike large industrial organizations, have no means of making surveys and negotiating for large blocks of power to be delivered to them at rates mutually satisfactory. When they have to depend upon organizations over which they have no control, their opportunity to make sure of receiving adequate and reliable power at low cost is very limited. But when they own and control their own generation and transmission and distribution system, they have a positive means of telling that their power requirements are met, and met in the most economical and satisfactory manner. Here, in this productive area, the farmers have taken this means of serving themselves and their neighbors so they need not fear that the indifference of their suppliers will cause them material loss and inconvenience."

When the speeches were over, the visitors toured the big new power plant. It is impressive above all in the way in which mechanization has been carried to a point at which machines do most of the work. Coal comes up the Mississippi by barge from mines in Illinois and Kentucky and, incidentally, at a price of $4.00 a ton compared with the price for hauling by rail of $8.00 a ton. It is unloaded by a large stationary crane and moved from a stock pile by power-driven equipment. From here it is taken to the crusher on a belt conveyer and carried to a large storage bunker near the top of the plant. From this point it flows down steel chutes into a pulverizer where it is ground as fine as flour dust. Mixed with preheated air, it burns at a temperature of approximately 2000 degrees Fahrenheit. From the twelve miles of boiler tubes steam at a pressure of 850 pounds per square inch is fed into the turbine and so power is generated. All through Dairyland's system this energy lifts, pulls, hauls, warms, and freezes for thousands of families in the great valley of the Mississippi. Yes, it is a monument. But it is more than a monument. It is a living and growing institution into which a great many Americans have put their hopes and convictions.

Iowa has always been inherently more conservative than Wisconsin, and it would be hard to imagine anyone more ruggedly Iowan than Ben Jaspers of Steamboat Rock. He sits behind the big plate-glass window of the Farmers Exchange Bank in Steamboat Rock hunched over the desk from which he runs not only the bank and much of the town but a great deal of the organized life of this part of Iowa. He is a Republican and, what is more, a conservative

Republican. I would imagine he agrees about ninety-five per cent of the time with the stand taken by the most conservative Republicans in Iowa's conservative delegation in Congress. Yet this is the man who has been largely responsible for pioneering rural electrification in Central Iowa and for initiating the first generating co-operative in the United States. (There are other claims to being first in the generating field.) As for Ben Jaspers, he sees nothing at all surprising in this. He and the other farmers wanted power on their farms and they had to get it at a low rate. Somebody had to take the lead. As he tells it, it is as simple as that.

Jaspers knew hardship as a boy. His father was a baker in North Germany who migrated to an Iowa farm. Four years after the boy, Ben, was born, his father died. During the next ten years Ben, an older brother, Henry, and their mother operated the family farm four and a half miles northeast of Steamboat Rock. Ben went to the East Clay Rural School and a little later he was the first graduate of the East Clay School to go to the Steamboat Rock High School. There were no consolidated school buses in those days and the boy often rode a ten-mile round trip on horseback across frozen fields with the wind blowing fiercely across the prairie. Working as a carpenter to pay his way, he went on with his education at Iowa State Teachers College at Cedar Falls and at the Central Iowa Business College at Marshalltown.

Jaspers had tried to get power for his farm. He had been rebuffed, as so many others had been, by the attitude of the private power companies. When the opportunity of REA came along, he was ready. Starting out himself to acquire the first right of way of three hundred miles, he worked intensely hard for a nominal salary and with no expense account.

Someone had to do the job. Jaspers had become one of the incorporators of the Hardin County electrification project in 1937. Recalling those days, he says he was just about everything—member of the board, secretary, temporary manager, working on the promotional and organizational end of the business. He served as project manager until 1944, learning all there is to know of the administrative side of the power distribution business and quite a lot about the technical side. When the Federated Co-operative Power Association of Hampton was merged with the Central Electric Federated Co-operative Association of Pocohantas to form the present Corn Belt Power Co-operative, Jaspers was named to head the new organization.

"Sure, it's work," he says, and he asks his secretary to get out the record of his service as head of the Corn Belt co-op in 1950. That record shows he gave sixty full days of service during that year. And this does not include part days, the secretary explained.

This conservative Iowa Republican recalls a visit that an executive of one of the private utility companies paid him about the time that Jaspers was advocating the necessity of starting a generating co-op in order to get power at a reasonable wholesale cost. There in the front window of the bank they had a talk which went somewhat as follows:

The utility executive: Now you're being forced into this power generating business, aren't you, Mr. Jaspers? That's pretty clear to me.

Jaspers: Yes, I guess that's about right. But who is forcing us into it?

Utility executive: You know very well who it is. It's the Rural Electrification Administration in Washington.

Jaspers: No, you're just dead wrong about that. It's you fellows with your two-cent rate that have forced us into it.

The wholesale rate, when the first generating co-op was started in February of 1937, was as high as 2.8 cents per kilowatt-hour, according to Jaspers. Yet if you talk about "public power," Ben Jaspers is against it. Some co-op leaders in Iowa would like to see the Government build transmission lines to bring power from the great Missouri River reclamation project into Iowa. Jaspers believes that a statewide generating system is essential for the three generating co-ops now in existence, with considerable development called for in the future, such a system to be linked in a sort of Midwest grid with Wisconsin's Dairyland Co-operative. Then that co-op grid would eventually be tied into the public power net that comes down from the Missouri Valley. But in the view of Jaspers and the Iowans who think like him, the link-up should be through transmission lines built by the co-operatives themselves.

Whether the explanation is the conservative background or the pragmatic Jaspers approach, in Iowa a most unusual union has occurred between co-operative power and private power. With a seven-million-dollar loan from REA the Central Iowa Power Co-operative built a 40,000-kilowatt plant near Cedar Rapids. The co-operative plant is to be operated by the Iowa Electric Light and Power Company. The power being distributed to 30,000 Iowa farm families living in an area extending from the banks of the Mississippi River to within a hundred miles of the Missouri is carried by the power company over its network of 115,000- and 34,500-volt transmission lines.

At the dedication of the new plant in June of 1950, the "wedding" was hailed as unique in America's industrial history. Rex Conn, farm editor of the Cedar Rapids *Gazette*, described the construction of the plant as occurring "within the framework of two types of private enterprise organizations. . . with help from the United States Government." J. S. Russell, farm editor of the Des Moines *Register* and *Tribune*, spoke of the union as "a degree of mutual confidence and co-operation which is a mark for everyone else to shoot at." Present as principals at this union were Fay E. Wilcox of the co-op and Sutherland Dows, head of the power company and a half-dozen other utilities which he owns virtually outright.

But many of those who ate a chicken dinner in the shadow of the big turbine generator could remember back to a time when things were not so harmonious between the representatives of private and co-operative power. The old-timers in particular had not forgotten that one of the Dows companies carried the issue of the right of a co-operative to generate and transmit electricity up through the Supreme Court of the state. That is why even such conservative co-operators as Ben Jaspers are concerned lest the younger generation take it all too much for granted. The younger generation did not know the struggle. They have fallen heir to a system that seems to work more or less effortlessly and for that matter almost automatically. It seems to go along with the prosperity that is so fresh and shiny and new almost everywhere you look in Iowa. In the midst of this prosperity they are constantly finding additional uses for electricity. Some of these uses have to be explained to the greenhorn from the city.

The farm of Governor William Beardsley was one of the very first in the state to be electrified with co-operative power. The governor was also one of the very first to use infrared lamps for heat in the hog houses in which his sows farrowed. Until the experimental use of artificial heat at Iowa State College, farrowing occurred necessarily in the spring, and if it was a late spring, the likelihood was for heavy losses in the litters. These losses were both from disease and from crushing as the sow, seeking warmth, rolled onto her young. In the modern farrowing house an infrared lamp is put up in one corner after the litter is born. Then a partition is so arranged that the piglets can get to the heat but the sow is kept away from that corner by the partition. This means greatly reduced losses. And it also means that farrowing time can be planned without too much regard for the weather.

Electricity has been adapted to specialized uses that the farmer of thirty or forty years ago would never have dreamed of. For example, on the mink farm of Al and Joe Stuekerjuergen power supplied by the Southeast Iowa Co-operative Electric Association does a variety of jobs. The nearly two thousand mink killed annually for their pelts are electrocuted in small cages wired for a 220-volt charge, which brings death almost instantly. Electrocution is considered much faster and more satisfactory than cyanide gas, which was formerly used. An oversized meat grinder, powered by a three-horsepower motor, grinds a hundred pounds of horsemeat a day. The meat goes into an electrically powered mixer where fish and cereal are added. With two thousand animals, each in a separate pen, the problem of providing water was burdensome until running water pumped through a hydrant system by electricity made it comparatively simple. Both pelts and reserves of food are stored in big electric freezers.

But mink farms are the exception. The rule is corn, and the power line goes into virtually every farm in Iowa to run machines both inside and outside the house, refrigerators, hay dryers, milking machines, grinders, that were rare or nonexistent two decades ago. As REA in Washington announced the addition of the three millionth farm family to get electric power, the IRECA *News*, published by the statewide co-operative association, suggested in January of 1950 that this may have been one of two hundred farm families connected to power lines in Iowa a month before. The Administration in Washington had explained that it would be impossible to identify a single farm without making a purely arbitrary choice. But the Iowa paper listed the families on whom this distinction might have fallen.

If you want to know how an individual farm family feels about it, talk to Mr. and Mrs. John Buscher of Dundee. For seven years on a rented farm they had electricity. Buscher even had a radio in his barn. Then they bought a run-down place and began to build it up. It was three years before the Buschers were able to get a connection on the lines of the Buchanan County Rural Electric Co-operative. "You have to go through what we did, to see what it means," says Buscher. "Why, it was liking stepping back into the Dark Ages!"

But the political challenge to REA is still lively in Iowa and elsewhere. The National Tax Equality Association continues to propagandize against all co-operatives. Other active and well-financed organizations such as the American Progress Foundation work to brand rural electrification as "socialistic." Right in the heart of the farming country which has benefited so greatly from the program, a local Lions Club was duped into adopting a resolution approving an amendment to the Constitution providing that "the Government of the United States shall not engage in any business, professional, commercial, or industrial enterprise with its citizens, except as specified in the Constitution." The members of the club appeared very surprised when they were told that such an amendment would kill the rural electrification loans, put the REA co-operatives out of business, and stop the sale of appliances by the stores in the town.

In neither Indiana nor Illinois have the distributing co-ops gone into generation and transmission. Relations with private power suppliers seem to be good. In Indiana this may be explained by the stick-behind-the-door psychology.

In 1949 thirteen co-ops in that state and one in Ohio formed the Hoosier Co-op Energy, Inc., which applied to REA for a loan for a generating plant. This was for a unit which with all substations and other essentials would cost about $50,000,000. It would be large enough to give all the co-ops a reserve of power and make them comparatively independent of the utilities. While this has never advanced beyond the preliminary stage, the file of facts and figures is increasing in bulk and it could be pushed at any time.

There is no apparent co-ordination between the political conservatism of a state and the public power issue, or not at any rate in the Midwest. Thus Nebraska, which is certainly as conservative as Indiana or Iowa, is by virtue of the adoption of a system of Public Power Districts virtually all public power. This is an extraordinary development which would require at least another chapter to describe in detail. In addition to the PPDs in Nebraska, there are ten REA co-ops.

Everywhere the common denominator is the necessity for more power. In Minnesota dairy herds are constantly increasing while at the same time milk regulations in the cities grow stricter. The latter mean the kind of handling and cooling possible only with electric power at low cost in volume. The argument over whether new generating facilities are necessary should long since have been shown to be utterly irrelevant. Yet it comes up again and again as the co-ops struggle for what is today an essential of farm production.

Chapter Nine
THE SOUTHWEST

IT MIGHT be the county fair or it could be that the circus had come to town. The crowd was in a holiday mood. People moved from tent to tent where the appliance dealers had set up their exhibits. Through the day the events of the program followed one after another: the 4-H Club demonstration, the baseball game, the drawing of prizes, the talent show.

This was the annual meeting of the Farmers Electric Cooperative of Newport. More than four thousand people had come in from all round the countryside and they stayed until the very end when the last fireworks were shot off. Not only were Buck Turner and his "REA Buckaroos" on the bandstand but every guitarist from three or four counties had come to compete in the talent show.

This annual meeting had been preceded by ten community meetings throughout the region served by the Newport co-op. One of the characteristics of the program in Arkansas, thanks to the leadership both at the statewide and the local level, is an organized effort to bring home to each member the importance of the co-op.

One feature of each of the community meetings is an REA forum of the air. Four contestants tell of the uses to which they put electricity and what their co-op means to them. The winner is awarded a table lamp, and each of the other contestants receives a carton of 100-watt lamps. The program is transcribed and later in the week broadcast over radio station KNBY. Likewise two fifteen-minute musical programs, made up of talent from the local community, are recorded for use over the radio the following week. Where consolidated schools have tended to break up the old sense of community feeling, these meetings are helping to restore it.

One of the gayest and most responsive groups is in Blackville, which name derives from the founder of the town rather than the fact that it is a Negro community. A leader in the community is Professor E. E. Kennerson. He put remarkable eloquence into his statement on the value of electricity, beginning, "If I had the wisdom of Socrates and the brilliance of Plato, I could not begin to tell you ..." Both white and Negro members take part in the Blackville meeting, and when Mrs. Carl Cross, wife of the manager of the Newport co-op, gives forth with swing at the piano the voices that come in on the chorus seem actually loud enough to bring down the roof.

At Newport the crowds spread out under the trees in the park had found the program entertaining enough through the day. But what they were really waiting for was the big event of the evening. That was the appearance of Governor Sid McMath. In Arkansas they take their politics seriously, and McMath had chosen to come out on the side of public power development.

Just how many people in the crowd understood the implications of this it would be impossible to say. But certainly for many of them the governor is a kind of hero. Young, almost boyish in appearance, he nevertheless has a stern set to his jaw, the look of a Jacksonian hero, which is a distinct political asset. When Sid speaks, the crowd sits silent except for an occasional yippee of approval.

The governor was speaking at Newport four days after the Arkansas Public Service Commission had handed down a decision in a case that had opened the power issue wide. Three distributing co-ops—the Arkansas Valley Electric of Ozark, the Carroll Electric of Berryville, and the Ozark Rural Electric of Fayettville—had joined to form the Arkansas Electric Co-operative Corporation. The new co-op had applied to REA for a loan of $10,500,000 for a steam-generating plant and transmission system to serve their members in Northwest Arkansas. This plant is to be operated by the co-op, but its entire output will be sold to the Southwestern Power Administration. In turn SPA will sell to the co-ops all the power their members need, even beyond the capacity of the plant. The transmission lines are also to be leased to the Southwestern Power Administration, a Department of the Interior agency that sells the power generated at federal dams in the Southwest.

The advantages of combining steam and hydroelectric plants have long been recognized in the power industry. One of the chief advantages is that a hydro plant produces both "firm" power that can be delivered day in and day out and secondary or "dump" power that can be delivered only a part of the time because the flow of water is not steady the year round. Obviously dump power is not worth as much as firm power, and anyone who can buy dump power cheaply and firm it up with steam generation is in an excellent position to make a good profit or to give consumers lower-cost electricity. Perhaps the most basic of all the issues in the SPA controversy is this: Who is going to control the dump power from these public hydro projects? The farmers see no reason why this publicly developed resource should be turned over exclusively to the power companies. Yet this is what will happen if the farm co-ops are prevented from building their own steam plants and transmission lines, since these are the means by which dump power can be converted into available low-cost power.

It was over the lease with the Southwestern Power Administration that the controversy boiled up furiously. In Washington and at Little Rock before the Public Service Commission the power companies intervened. Under the lease SPA will take all of the steam-generated power from the plant to be built at Ozark and merge it with its own hydroelectric power. Thanks to the steady inflow of steam power into its system, SPA will have a much greater volume of firm power.

The Arkansas Electric co-op, for its part, will get all the power it needs, and will need, from this source. Both REA and Interior approved the lease agreement. The last hurdle was the State Public Service Commission, it was hoped.

As with most state utility commissions, in Arkansas both employees and commissioners are underpaid. Engineers, who receive in the neighborhood of $4000 a year, are constantly being hired away by private utilities. It is hardly surprising that they look to the utilities for future opportunity. Commissioners are paid $5000 a year. To say that the commission sits on an Olympian peak divorced from politics would be a gross exaggeration.

The new co-op had filed its application on January 30, 1951. On August 10 the commission handed down its decision. Two of the commissioners, John R. Thompson and C. Howard Gladden, decided in favor of permitting the co-op to go ahead with the generating plant. The chairman, Scott Wood, wrote a minority opinion in which he held that federal law does not authorize two federal agencies to enter into such an arrangement. The majority opinion, with its frequent references to statements made in the commission hearings that went on from March through June, is an interesting document.

One line taken by the power companies in this controversy was that the basic Arkansas law granting co-operatives the right to function in areas of the state carefully set apart from other areas allocated to the private power companies does not cover generating and transmission systems which might encroach on the territory of the companies. The majority found that there had been no effort on the part of the three distribution co-ops to invade the territory of the power company or to try to take away their customers. The opinion declared:

"This legislation in our opinion clearly contemplated that the method used in securing a power supply is incidental to the fundamental purpose of supplying electric power to the unserved farms of Arkansas. At the time this legislation was adopted, less than three per cent of the farms in Arkansas had electric service. This splendid record of accomplishment is a tribute to both the rural electric co-operatives and the intervening power company. We conclude that the General Assembly did not intend to limit or restrict the method that would be employed in accomplishing the basic objective of bringing electric service to the farms of Arkansas."

Much of the stress by the opposition had been put on the working of the Federal Flood Control Act of 1944. It was argued that the language of that act excluded any such teaming up by the government agencies alleged to be in competition with private power suppliers. But the majority declared that if Congress wanted to change the law by narrowing it down so that such an operation could be excluded, Congress had the right to do so. As the majority opinion pointed out, representatives of the power company had been repeatedly appearing before congressional committees urging such changes.

And most important of all, the majority found that the new co-operative would supply power to its member co-ops "at a cost below the present charges of the intervening power company or below any offer of the intervening power company." The opinion declared: "Under the laws of this state and under the showing in this hearing, we cannot deny the farmers in this area the privilege of building their own facilities to serve themselves, and by such denial require that they take power from the intervening power company. We are of the opinion that the general public will be materially aided by the construction of the facilities proposed in this petition, and more particularly the rural people in the northwest part of Arkansas, and that no great harm will be suffered by anyone, and that the general economy of the state will be promoted by such construction."

In his minority opinion Chairman Wood declared that there was no congressional authority which can be "stretched by the most liberal construction . . . to authorize SPA to buy power for the purpose of selling it or to construct plants to generate power by steam for the purpose of selling such power." He pointed out that the records show that the power administration had asked Congress to make appropriations of $21,000,000 for the construction of steam-generating plants and that Congress had denied the request. Wood said the records showed that other co-operatives in Arkansas planned to follow the same course. Disagreeing with the majority, he found that co-ops were presently paying "one of the lowest rates in the country," which he said was less than the rate they would have to pay for power purchased under the proposed contract with SPA.

But while the lawyers and the experts might argue over the legalisms and the technicalities, for most people in Arkansas this dispute had become highly personalized. On the one side stand Governor McMath and the co-operative leaders. On the other side is C. Hamilton Moses, for many years president of the Arkansas Power and Light Company, a former law partner of the late Senator Joe Robinson, and a commanding figure in the state. Moses is no mean adversary, being for one thing reputed the best Sunday-school teacher in the Southwest, and in Arkansas that counts for a great deal. He is tireless at meetings and rallies, holding forth wherever a few are gathered together with skill and persuasiveness. Moses is handicapped in that his company is wholly owned and controlled in New York. The eminent Arkansas citizens he names to his board of directors, including two retired preachers, are largely window dressing.

Moses has always said that he does not oppose REA co-operatives in the business of distributing electric power to farmers for their own use. The propaganda his company widely disseminates fights what Moses calls the "master co-op." Presumably this is a generating and transmission co-operative. Or at any rate it is a generating co-op that in any way encroaches on the "right" of a private utility to supply wholesale power to all REA-financed co-ops.

At one point Moses proposed to several of the co-operatives long-term contracts for power at a low rate. As co-operative leaders tell the story, they shied away from this offer. The reason? Well, such contracts might work all right for two or three years and be satisfactory to everybody concerned. But then supposing a group of consumers in the city should intervene with the Public Service Commission, protesting because of the low wholesale rate paid by the co-ops and arguing that the city users were in effect subsidizing the rate? The commission could thereupon invalidate the contract. Indeed, Moses had once filed with the commission an application to raise the rate in a contract between his company and a co-op. Thus, since politics and influence can never be entirely ruled out, the co-ops felt that they would later be at the mercy of private power suppliers sooner or later.

Although the power companies have now carried the issue to the courts, construction of the steam plant will probably proceed. A 30,000-kilowatt generating station, it will be almost the only large steam plant in the state designed to burn coal. The majority on the Arkansas Public Service Commission pointed out that this would be a distinct advantage, since the plant will be located in an area of large coal reserves. Because of this fact the cost of coal to the co-op will be competitive with the cost of natural gas to the more recently built power plants of the Arkansas Power and Light Company.

Some of all this was in what Sid McMath had to say as he stood under the floodlights on the platform while the crowd sat patiently in the warm darkness. Needless to say, it was translated into language that these Arkansas farmers and their families could understand. This was politics dealing with an issue vital to the people of the state, an issue with sensitive nerve centers reaching back not only into Little Rock but Washington, where Arkansas is powerfully represented. Only two months before, John R. Steelman, assistant to the President, had come back to be hailed in his native state and to accompany Clyde Ellis on a speaking tour before several co-ops.

Neither the construction of the plant nor the decision of the court will end the controversy. Moses keeps alive the possibility that he will take this issue before the people by becoming a candidate for governor. Many of the weekly newspapers in which the power company generously distributes its advertisements have been calling on him to become a candidate. He is particularly proud of one captioned, "A Moses to Lead Us."

In at least one phase this controversy touches on the future of the whole state. Moses argues that there is no power shortage in Arkansas; that, quite to the contrary, there is a surplus of power. Co-op leaders take just the opposite position. They cite power outages and a deficiency in many communities which have curtailed the use of electricity. The fact is that very few defense industries were located in Arkansas in World War II, nor have there been many established there during the current rearmament effort. Whether this has been due to a lack of power is a matter of debate.

It is a fact, however, that the state commission determined, and the power companies did not deny, that the state was using more power than was being generated within its borders. It is also true that at the very time the companies were opposing the co-op plant as unnecessary, Arkansas Power and Light filed an application with the commission to build a substantially larger plant stating that it was necessary.

At one time the Atomic Energy Commission contemplated putting the hydrogen bomb plant in the state. But it would have been necessary to build additional power facilities, and whether they could have been built coincidental with the construction of the huge bomb plant is highly questionable. Governor McMath has pointed out that Arkansas's potential and actual production of electric power vary greatly, and failure to develop this power potential will seriously hamper the state's progress.

The bitterness in the controversy goes back into the past. Those on the public power side blame the utility companies and their insistent opposition for the fact that at the outset of the New Deal a "little TVA" was not constructed on Arkansas's White River. They say that the plans were all prepared in Washington and that opposition in the state sidetracked the proposal. Some of the dams originally proposed are now being built by the federal Government. The Norfolk dam went into operation in 1945. Bull Shoals, which will be the fifth largest concrete dam in the world, will begin to generate power in 1952.

Sometimes, in a philosophic mood, the co-operative leaders are inclined to be thankful for Ham Moses. "Without Ham we would never have organized as intensively as we have," they say. "Without him we never would have been on our toes." Certainly it has been a fierce fight in recent years, with the co-ops struggling to get a toehold in power production, which they consider essential to their independent existence and as insurance for reasonable rates.

Harry Oswald, formerly with REA in Washington, and later in Arkansas, is manager of the co-ops' state association. He has searched out many ways to save money for the co-ops, organizing a repair plant at the Little Rock headquarters which has already demonstrated substantial economies on co-op repair bills for transformers and other equipment. Harry originated the idea of having the co-ops hold their annual meetings in series, which allowed a traveling electric show to visit each meeting in turn. Like other state managers he spends about half his time on the road, knowing every line and almost every insulator in the territory served by the co-operatives.

With the new resort development that has come with the lakes created by the new dams, there is a rapidly expanding market for power. Arkansas Power and Light is pushing a large expansion program. But Oswald and the other co-operators are convinced that all the plans now on the drawing board or in process of construction will fall short of future needs. They say that power company estimates of future needs have always been too low. The changing pattern of rural life in Arkansas will mean greater demands for current than anyone has foreseen. And these men who have given so much of their time and their effort to the task of rural electrification want to make sure that farm co-operators have a part in the future development of an enterprise that is almost as vital to them as the land itself.

As might be expected, farther to the Southwest, Texas pride and Texas independence are part of the story of rural electrification in the state that talks like a continent. Those qualities are particularly conspicuous among the men who have worked so hard to make a success of the Brazos River Transmission Electric Co-operative organized by several distribution co-ops. Powerful forces, both political and economic, conspired to block and delay the development of power resources and transmission lines that were vital if Texas farmers were to get sufficient power for full production.

In many respects the story is a familiar one. The power companies, with Texas Power and Light in the lead, argued that there was no need for further generating facilities. Transmission lines would duplicate those of the private companies. As has happened repeatedly, the utilities underestimated future power needs. Shortages would today be far more serious if it had not been for the determined efforts of co-operatives, in the face of equally determined opposition, to build facilities to supply their own power needs.

The contest in Texas became extremely bitter. The utilities in paid advertisements attacked the co-op with the familiar smear words. When the co-op sought to reply, some newspapers refused their ads until vigorous protest brought a change of heart and the paid reply was run.

The farmers and ranchers backing the Brazos project were not to be stopped. In their individual distributing co-ops they had been through a lengthy and in most instances futile effort to get low-cost power. The original thirteen co-ops that formed the Brazos River project in February of 1941 had been paying, on the average, fifteen mills per kw-h for electric power.

One of them was the Bartlett County Electric Co-operative, which claims to be the first distributing co-op organized in the United States. Bartlett today has complete area coverage in the fertile Blackland and Grand Prairie regions, producing cotton, corn, oats, grain, sorghums, wheat, peanuts, peaches, pears, and various truck crops. W. R. Janke, who was elected first president of the board of directors and still serves in that capacity, recalls that he and two others put up fifty dollars of their own money for the charter. They had been trying to get a private company to serve them and had been told not only that the company would not do it but that it could not be done at all.

After Bartlett got a loan to build a distributing system, the utilities in the area refused to give the co-op a wholesale rate. They proposed to charge their regular retail rate. In turn they were informed by R. W. Miller, Bartlett's manager and later to become manager of the Brazos project, that a generating plant would be built to serve the farmers in the area. At that point the companies decided that the lowest sale price for wholesale power would be fifteen mills per kw-h. That price was maintained until the distribution co-ops in the Brazos watershed began negotiations for a loan to build a transmission system. The cost was then reduced to twelve mills and when approval of the loan was announced, it dropped to nine.

The co-op leaders who formed the Brazos project wanted to get low-cost power from the Brazos River Conservation and Reclamation District, a state authority, and from the Possum Kingdom Dam on the Brazos River near Mineral Wells. The latter was authorized by President Roosevelt with $4,500,000 of WPA funds in 1937.

In March of 1941 the power companies met at Temple to oppose the proposed contract between the Brazos district and the Brazos co-op. At that meeting another reduction was announced which lowered the rate to approximately six mills. When in 1949 the district and the co-op were in conflict over rates, partly as a result of political conniving in the state legislature, Manager Miller could say:

"There have been other reductions in wholesale power rates since the transmission co-operative began operations, and these reductions have extended to practically all of the distribution co-operatives in the state of Texas, and are now resulting in a savings to the farmers of Texas, who own and control these co-operatives, of more than a million dollars annually in wholesale power rates. The proof that this competition has been the motivating reason for reducing the costs of wholesale power is found in the fact that the other privately owned utility companies within this state are paying more for their wholesale power than the co-operative."

At the time the Brazos project was organized, the distribution co-ops were not getting adequate service. This was largely because the companies lacked adequate facilities to serve rural loads that were constantly expanding. Since they were unwilling to provide those facilities, the co-operatives themselves were forced to seek their own sources of power. According to a report filed with the state legislature by E. D. H. Farrow, president of the Brazos Co-operative, that condition continued into 1949 when numerous farm homes did not have sufficient refrigeration or could not operate a water pump and a radio at the same time.

The war had caused long delays in line construction even after all contracts were signed. Nevertheless Farrow could point out that Brazos had been able to meet its operating expenses, repay the Government its obligation, and maintain a reserve required under the contract between power district and co-op. That reserve in 1949 was $109,150.

In June of that year Brazos obtained a new REA loan of $6,480,000 to increase its power resources and extend its lines. This would expand the steam plant built at the end of the war and named after Representative Bob Poage of Texas, one of the most steadfast friends of REA in Congress. The plant, near Belton, was to have two new 11,500-kw steam-generating units installed to increase the total capacity to 34,500 kw. In addition to its own plant, Brazos obtains power from the Morris Sheppard Dam, owned and operated by the Brazos district, the Southwestern Power Administration, the Lower Colorado River Authority, and the Texas Power and Light Company. Studies by engineers for REA and Brazos leading up to the loan showed rapid increases in power needs building up to a kilowatt-hour requirement for the nineteen co-operative members of 193,800,000 in 1953 and 308,750,000 in 1958.

The dispute before the state legislature was in part over the right of the Federal Power Commission to determine the rates to be paid by the Brazos co-op to the Brazos district. "The Brazos co-operative," said Farrow in his statement to the legislature, "is a free, private, taxpaying business enterprise. It is a Texas-owned business. No Federal 'gifts' or 'grants' involved.

"The rural electrification program," Farrow declared, "while bringing untold benefits to the rural people of our state, has not cost the taxpayers one cent. Texas co-operatives are more than a million dollars ahead of schedule in their repayments on their loans."

This strong sense of independence is typical of those who direct the Brazos project. Sitting in on a directors' meeting in Fort Worth, you know that these are men from the wide open spaces who have an inherent distrust of dictation and dependence. One after the other they tell of early struggles over power rates and of how, dramatically and swiftly, the utilities offered reductions when once it was obvious that these Texans intended to go through with a plan that they felt had been forced upon them.

The last annual report showed that Brazos had in service at the end of June 1951, 802 miles of transmission line, and 121 additional miles of line already built and to be energized in succeeding months will complete the southeastern and northeastern loops of the transmission system. The co-op serves the city of Caldwell with a minimum of 400 kw. It also wheels power over its lines for delivery to a private distributing system for which it receives $6480 annually from the Texas Power and Light Company. Brazos's headquarters at Waco are now located in a handsome new air-conditioned building designed with the simplicity of line and the skillful use of color that distinguish electric co-op buildings throughout the country.

The dedication of the Bob Poage steam plant at Belton in March of 1950 was in many ways an historic occasion. Present were not only the directors of the co-operative and many co-op members, but George Beams, vice-president of the Texas Power and Light Company and Douglas G. Wright, administrator of the Southwestern Power Administration. In his speech Poage passed around the pipe of peace. This, he said, was the symbolic end of the fussing and the feuding. The contract with Texas Power and Light was, said Poage, like the utility's contract with SPA. The three forces in the power picture were now in perfect integration. Everybody had the right to carry on his own business. But everybody had to stay in line, because if they stepped out of line they could be disciplined by one of the competing forces.

The Brazos project has helped make it possible to overcome the problem of the great distances separating ranch homes and to reach one of the major goals of rural electrification—area coverage. They are proud in Texas of the way in which this goal is being achieved in spite of the handicaps. The outstanding success story in this department is that of the Southwest Texas Electric Co-operative.

Not long after passage of the REA Act seven very determined men in Schleicher County began to organize a co-operative. Schleicher County is west of Fort McKavett, farther west and more Texan, as the editor of the statewide paper put it, than even a movie script writer could imagine. The seven determined organizers talked with every rancher in the county's 1331 square miles. They knew they would have to sign up every ranch if they were to have a chance of getting an REA loan. A few were skeptical, but as E. C. Hill says, these finally paid the five-dollar membership fee if only to end the argument. With B. W. Chesser of REA's applications and loans division they surveyed the area, saving time by mapping out the location of members from the vantage point of the windmills visible for many miles in this high plains area. They secured right-of-way easements for line building; sometimes, in the case of absentee landowners, paying for the easements from their own pockets in cash. A loan application was completed.

If they had known at that point how long was the road ahead, the seven ranchers might have given up. REA at that time put great stress on density of population. And the newly formed co-op was applying for a loan to build 192 miles on line to serve only 182 members. What amazed REA in Washington was that this represented 100 per cent of the rural population of Schleicher County. The loan was turned down on the ground that it could never pay out.

As an alternative, REA suggested the possibility of consolidating with a co-op being formed in neighboring Kimble County. Another application was worked up but the result was the same: too few people for so much line. The organizers were still not discouraged. Altogether they worked up a total of six different applications in the course of which they pointed out that the average income of ranchers in the county was twice the average in the state. Almost every ranch home already had running water, plumbing, electric refrigeration, and other appliances, all run by costly Diesel generating units. Enclosed with the later applications were guarantees by members to pay high monthly minimums, one rancher guaranteeing seventy-five dollars a month and others fifty dollars. An REA expert came from Washington to verify these remarkable statements and he found they were all true.

By the time the loan was at last approved, the war was on and the co-op could not proceed with construction. In January of 1945 the first contract for construction was let and in April of that year the work of building 232 miles of line to serve 202 members began. Current flowed over the first lines the following January. As a result of expansion into Menard and Tom Green counties the co-op today has 582 meters on a 921-mile system.

The same story of area coverage has been repeated in many places in the state. The Floyd County Rural Electric Co-operative in the south high plains has in less than fifteen years completed coverage in seven counties with some 1350 miles of line and 2068 member homes receiving power. There, too, the first organizers were told they had no chance of getting a loan or making an electric co-operative pay out. They had previously offered a private utility $6000 in cash to extend a line into the county and had been told that the company was not interested. Since 1938 a total of twelve loans have been made in the amount of $2,619,000.

Each time a farm community was energized it was a major event. In one community that did not have Diesel plants most families had installed refrigerators, washing machines, and so on long in advance of the great day. They agreed that the night after the lines were energized they would meet and exchange experiences. One woman had saved up the washing for two weeks to try out her washing machine. Another reported on how an electric dishwasher simplified her life. But the prize went to an older woman who said, "Well, we just turned on the light and looked at each other—it was the first time I'd seen Pa after dark in thirty years."

The last tribe of Indians intact in Texas, the Alabamas, get power from the Sam Houston Electric Co-operative. So do a few remaining Coushattas also living on the only reservation in the state in Polk County. It is singularly fitting that these four hundred Indians should be served by the Sam Houston co-op, since it was Sam Houston who first befriended them in 1854 after they had been pushed from place to place as the white man swiftly took over the new country. Through his efforts they got the first 1280 acres of their present reservation. The Sam Houston co-op now serves nearly every family on the reservation. The Reverend Oscar Landry, the Presbyterian missionary, has helped to wire each house that stands on its own plot of from two to ten acres of land.

With the wide diversity of climate in Texas' far-spreading borders, co-op members find many uses for electric power. The Magic Valley Electric Co-operative in the lower Rio Grande Valley provides power that grades, washes, dries, and waxes citrus fruits for shipment to every part of the country. Manager Mel Perry of the Magic Valley Groves, a typical citrus farm, has installed two hundred infrared frost lights to protect his papaya and coconut trees from a sudden drop in temperature. He plans to extend this system of protection to his citrus groves, thereby replacing the cumbersome method of lighting smudges in advance of a frost warning. When the mercury drops to thirty-four, an automatic alarm system sets off a warning.

Irrigation wells are operated with power supplied by the Rita Blanca Electric Co-operative in Dallam, Hartley, Moore, and Sherman counties, which were carved out of the vast XIT Ranch. The state of Texas granted the syndicate that built the capitol building at Austin three million acres of land. In 1882 the land was stocked with cattle and fenced with barbed wire as the XIT Ranch. That barbed wire was a challenge to Texas ranchers, who believed that the wide open spaces were meant to stay open. There were fierce battles between rustlers, amateur and professional, and the trigger-happy cowhands of XIT. But that is long since past and today wells and electric pumps pour water onto wheat and alfalfa fields. President of the co-op is Asa Willis, who had as much to do with getting the system started as any single individual. One well on Willis's farm five miles east of Texline flows approximately nine thousand gallons of water a minute with a thirty-horsepower electric motor and an eight-inch pump.

The electric co-operatives in Texas have an effective statewide organization called the Texas Power Reserve Electric Co-operative. Faced with what were considered exorbitant prices and a continuing shortage of poles in 1944, the association got an REA loan for the purchase of a pole-processing plant. In early 1951 the last payment was made on that loan, and as the statewide paper, *Texas Co-op Power*, observed, it became "strictly a home-owned and -operated institution." In a ceremony at the NRECA convention in Cleveland, Administrator Wickard received the final check from Allen Burditt, president of the statewide.

General manager of the statewide, editor of the paper and manager of the pole-processing plant is Elmo Osborne. That is a heavy load of responsibility for a young man of twenty-six, only five years out of the Marines. But Osborne has shown that he is more than able to handle it, thereby illustrating the way in which capable leadership has been called forth when the need arises. Young Osborne lived out most of the depression on his grandfather's farm near Abilene in West Texas. Water for drinking and all other purposes was hauled from nearly three miles away on a sledge drawn by a mule. The water in those barrels lasted two or three days and at the end of that time it was pretty warm and stale. He recalls that every day in his school lunch box for at least two years he had fried rabbit. You could always shoot rabbits. There is no bitterness in this recollection. But Osborne and the others who have come into another era are determined that it will never be like that again if they can help it—and they mean to help it.

In the member co-ops and in the statewide organization in Texas there is a generous share of rebel independence. Perhaps in no other state was there such resentment when REA announced a requirement that "prevailing wages" be paid by contractors performing construction work for co-ops using government loan funds. REA had no legal right to do it, so the Texans argued. This is our enterprise, they said, and so long as we make our payments on time no one can tell us how to run our own business. They suspected some kind of deal between the Department of Agriculture and the Department of Labor under which workers in the co-ops would be organized as an opening wedge for union organization in Texas, a state which is largely unorganized.

Co-operative leaders in Texas did not want to be used by labor, regardless of their feelings on trade unions. Their spokesman talked of the fear that unions might want the Government, through REA, to coerce the entry of unionization. They sent their vigorous protests both to REA and to their friends in Congress.

In Washington Georgia's powerful Senator Russell took up the cause of the Texas co-ops, calling on Wickard to explain his reasons for adopting the prevailing wage policy. Wickard explained that this policy had dated from the early years of the program, and had been dropped in 1948 only because a personnel shortage had made it impossible to administer. Labor unions, Wickard said, had sharply criticized REA for the policy's abandonment, and had urged Wickard to reinstate the prevailing wage formula. Failure to do so, the unions made clear, could mean the loss of organized labor's sorely needed support in the bitter generation-and-transmission fights of years to come.

The heat of this controversy has been dissipated largely through the fact that today most co-ops are more interested in wage ceilings than wage minimums. Also, Senator Russell, speaking for many representatives from agricultural states, impressed upon Wickard that he has no statutory authority for the establishment of a prevailing wage, and that such a policy would endanger the farmers' ability to build power lines. Wickard, unable to enforce his stand, still believes that in the long run inferior wages will be detrimental to the REA program.

In neighboring Oklahoma the record shows a long dispute between Southwestern Power Administration and two large private utilities, the Public Service Company of Oklahoma and the Oklahoma Gas and Electric Company. Frequently the co-ops found themselves caught in the middle of that quarrel, unable to get sufficient power at the same time that utility opposition blocked the building of additional facilities.

Early in 1950 the controversy was compromised by a contract approved by Administrator Wright and the Secretary of the Interior for SPA and the two utilities. Under this contract the hydro power of SPA was integrated with the steam-generated power of the utilities. Through this combined system the volume of firm power available was greatly increased. According to many observers in Oklahoma, the state will be in a much better position to attract industry. The Tulsa *Tribune*, which regards the postal system as a heinous invasion of private enterprise, wrote a sympathetic account of the interchange agreement as the first union of public and private power for the mutual benefit of all concerned.

But this contract, arrived at after months of negotiations, is only a compromise of irreconcilable positions. Douglas Wright, head of SPA, does not claim that the contract is the best one for the co-ops, but the best that could be negotiated at the present time. Wright had been instructed by Congress to attempt to negotiate contracts with private companies for the wheeling of government power. Furthermore, Wright, whose SPA operation has been in jeopardy every day of its life, had to distribute his power or face the threat of liquidation. Each year the southwestern power companies have urged Congress to liquidate the SPA, claiming it served no useful purpose.

While the contract for Oklahoma was under consideration, Clyde Ellis, executive manager of NRECA, opposed it as being against the long-term interests of the co-ops. Such contracts, Ellis explained, are wrong in principle. First of all, no wheeling arrangements are permanent in nature, or offer the co-ops a secure wholesale power supply. The unfriendly attitude of the power companies toward the co-ops, Ellis argued, and the presence of the State Utility Commission make these contracts flimsy things indeed.

Specifically, Ellis found many clauses of the Oklahoma contract against the best interests of the co-ops. The executive manager of NRECA contended that it was not nearly so favorable for co-ops as was the Texas contract. The Texas contract referred to a similar agreement that had been made between SPA and Texas Power and Light Company, covering a much smaller area. First of all, Ellis said, there was no State Utility Commission in Texas to abrogate the contract. Secondly, if the power companies refused to serve the co-ops at their load centers, how would SPA power reach the vast areas of Oklahoma in which the two power companies did not operate? Due in large part to Ellis's opposition to many clauses of this contract, changes favorable to the co-ops were incorporated in the final draft.

The final draft of the contract was accepted by a majority of Oklahoma co-operatives. And so through different viewpoints honestly presented a compromise was reached. The struggle has often been intense in the Southwest; and in Missouri, as is related in a later chapter, it is still acute. But one thing is shown beyond any doubt. That is the value of competition in bringing down rates and in expanding power resources.

Chapter Ten
THE NORTHWEST

ELECTRIC power is to the Northwest what oil is to the Southwest or coal to the East. The swiftly flowing streams and the great rivers that run down to the Pacific are a source of enormous energy, only a small fraction of which has as yet been harnessed. That energy is the focus of a new industrial and agricultural empire that is rapidly coming into being on the Pacific slope.

Smaller dam sites were developed by the private utilities or by city-owned systems. But the great reservoirs of power, the Columbia river 1200 miles in length and the Snake 1000 miles long, had to wait federal development through multi-purpose dams. This was beyond any private interest. Even against the background of the West—the snow-capped mountains, the great stands of timber, a sense of space and openness—dams such as the Grand Coulee and Bonneville have a grandeur of their own. Imagine, says the guide at Grand Coulee, the Empire State Building with its windows chinked up laid across the river and you will visualize the size of this dam. Niagara is dwarfed by the rush of water that comes down over the 360-foot-high spillway at Coulee when the banks of the Columbia are full.

When the work began on Grand Coulee Dam in 1934, the power companies violently opposed its construction. Calling the dam "a white elephant on the Columbia," they demanded to know what the power would ever be used for. Again in 1946 they called for a halt to any further development of the hydroelectric projects which, they claimed, would be a waste of money with power going begging.

As late as 1951 they again said there was plenty of power. Yet in that same year the Northwest faced the most serious shortage in the country. Charles E. Wilson, the defense mobilizer, served notice that unless some adjustment could be made, it might be necessary to compel aluminum companies to move their plants from that region. The only alternative seemed to be a widespread brown-out that would dim lights throughout the Pacific Northwest.

The news of the brown-out sent a wave of shock through the area. From almost every quarter came the demand to push construction still in progress on McNary, Hungry Horse, Chief Joseph, Detroit, and the other dams on the Columbia and its tributaries. There was a sudden and heightened realization that the future of the Northwest depends more and more on the vital energy that can be taken from the waters running down to the sea. A drought which lasted for ninety-four days in 1951 had drastically reduced the stream flow which made the power shortage all the more acute. In the background of this situation was the persistent failure to appreciate the growth of power demands and the constant opposition by private utilities to further expansion. The new industries, aluminum, chemical, and metallurgical plants, shipyards, and the atomic energy development—all depend on the white coal that can be transported almost instantly over the far-flung lines. If the Northwest is to maintain its industrial gains of the war and postwar years, power facilities will have to be expanded at a greater rate than before.

The farmer, too, is dependent on this source of energy to develop the vast farm space of the Northwest in the pattern of ever-growing fruitfulness and productivity. The key to rural electrification in the Northwest has been "Bonneville power" and the postage-stamp rate, a rate that is the same wherever power is delivered, regardless of the distance from the source.

Long before the power of the Columbia was available, farmers tried to get central station service. Here was the familiar story. They got nowhere when they asked the private utilities to extend their lines into the country.

But in the Northwest, and particularly in the state of Washington, an organization was ready at hand in the Grange. In Washington's thirty-nine counties there are seven hundred Granges which work through the county-wide Pomona, the state and national organization. With subsidiaries providing fire, life, and auto insurance; with wholesale markets and supply co-operatives in nearly every town in the state, the Grange is closely integrated into the whole economy.

Since 1890 Grange leaders had watched the cities of Centralia, Takoma, Ellenburg, Seattle, Eugene, and McMinnville operate successful municipal power plants. They had observed the genius of J. D. Ross as he built City Light of Seattle into one of the most successful utility operations in America. Ross worked on the theory that the cheaper you made electricity, the more people would buy. When he went to work for City Light in 1902, electricity cost twenty-three cents a kilowatt-hour in Seattle. By 1930, through Ross's efforts, the cost had been reduced to five cents a kilowatt-hour and the monthly use had gone to 100 kilowatt-hours per average household, perhaps the highest in the country. Why not, the Grange leaders asked, have counties operate electric systems in the same way that municipalities did? In that way electric lines could be extended into the country. This was the origin of the public utility district, or, as Oregon calls them, Peoples Utility District.

Largely through the efforts of the Grange in organizing Washington farmers, a law permitting public utility districts to be formed was passed in 1930. Under this law a majority of a county's voters can approve the creation of a public utility district, or PUD, as they are familiarly known. At the same election three commissioners are chosen to direct the operation of the county-wide PUD.

These commissioners have the power to purchase, condemn, or lease the properties of all private power companies operating in the district. Being a local unit of government, the PUD can exercise the right of eminent domain and levy certain taxes.

But Washington farmers found that this was a cumbersome way of getting their farms electrified. It was slow work obtaining the approval of the voters. Negotiating the sale, or condemnation and sale, of the property of the commercial power companies involved prolonged court battles. Aroused by the PUD movement, the companies, according to the Federal Power Commission, spent over a million dollars to defeat the program.

The result was that by 1935 few farm households were connected with central station service. The farmer was not especially concerned with methods. What he wanted was power.

Therefore, he turned hopefully to the federal rural power program and the co-operative approach. Today private power companies, public utility districts, and co-ops are all supplying Washington farmers with electricity. The co-ops and the PUDs have both done an excellent job of rural electrification. Both have borrowed from the REA in Washington. Both are nonprofit methods by which individuals in association may provide themselves with electric service. But there is an important distinction between them. The PUD is an agency of government with a majority of voters residing in a county deciding upon who shall provide them with electricity. The co-operative is a nonprofit private business which cannot condemn property or exercise a statuatory right of eminent domain or levy taxes. And while not restricted by county boundaries, the co-op may serve only rural areas not already provided with electric service.

The difference in service provided by the two is largely a matter of management and direction. As have the co-ops, PUDs also have suffered from inefficient managers or from an indifferent board of directors with a narrow outlook on rural electrification. Presumably since PUDs serve both towns and rural areas they should be able to provide lower average rates for the farmer. But with the Bonneville Power Administration selling power at the postage-stamp rate to all wholesale users the difference is negligible.

Friction between the PUDs and the electric co-ops at one point in the thirties threatened to break out in a full-fledged quarrel. They were in many respects rivals and the arguments for one approach or the other were hot and heavy. That dispute has since ceased to be a disruptive factor. The co-ops and the PUDs work together for certain common aims in the Northwest Public Power Association, one of the most lively and alert organizations of its kind in America.

Formed in 1940, the NWPPA was at first a loose confederation of public power leaders interested in the wholesaling of Columbia River power and concerned over the anti-public power attitude of certain wartime government agencies, conspicuously the Office of Production Management. By 1947 it included thirty-two member systems, among them several co-operatives. Leaders in the association felt it had grown large enough to incorporate.

Chosen as executive secretary of this association was a young man named Gus Norwood. It was one of those rare and fortunate instances of the right man in the right job. In a remarkably short time Norwood, with his drive and energy and above all his capacity for organization, has transformed NWPPA from what was largely a paper association to a dynamic force in the Pacific Northwest.

His is a kind of success story such as does not often get told. Brought up in a small town in Illinois where his father was a railroad man, Norwood had from early youth a great urge for education, knowledge. But in 1935 when he was ready for college, the family had few resources for further education. Gus applied for and won an appointment to the Naval Academy at Annapolis. In his first half year he was among the first fifteen in his class but thereafter he made a deliberate choice to extend the field of his study beyond the closely circumscribed curriculum rather than to concentrate on the competition for marks. Graduated in 1939, he fought in the war across the Pacific, taking part in the Doolittle raid on Tokyo, the Battle of Midway, and the island-hopping campaign. By 1946 he had risen to the rank of lieutenant-commander.

But Norwood did not want to make the Navy his permanent career. Retiring in 1946, he went back to school, this time to Harvard and a graduate course in public utility management at Harvard's famed Littauer Center. At the end of the year at Harvard he stepped into the NWPPA job, which was exactly what he wanted.

The broad purpose of the association is to bring together all types of public and co-operative power systems, to approach the question of power and natural resources on a regional basis, and to give balanced consideration to both operating and policy-making problems. In achieving these ends Norwood has stressed the principle of home rule. He wants the member systems to remain self-reliant and autonomous and not to throw their responsibilities and problems on the NWPPA. In accord with this belief, Norwood has kept the staff of the association to two persons—himself and a part-time secretary.

But he dedicates enough energy and thought to the job for at least a half-dozen people. This is above all on the side of efficient and thorough organization, which he constantly stresses. The president of the association, for example, is elected six months before he takes office and in that six months he studies every detail of the task for the coming year. Months of planning go into association meetings so that little or no time is wasted and the greatest possible benefit comes out of every moment of the session.

Perhaps the chief concern of the NWPPA is the full development of the power resources of the Northwest rivers. Only in that way, the association argues, can the growth of the Northwest empire continue with greater productivity on the farms and new industries to provide jobs for a rapidly growing population. This has brought the association into conflict with the salmon fishing interests that oppose dam building on the Columbia because they claim it keeps the salmon from moving upstream to spawn. But Norwood replies that the innocent salmon is being used as a monkey wrench by a "small and ruthless group" to paralyze hydroelectric development. And he points to the fish ladders at Bonneville up which some eight million salmon have climbed. The trouble with the salmon industry, according to the NWPPA, is ruthless and lawless overfishing at the mouth of the Columbia.

The association has also been in conflict with the Bureau of Reclamation. The difference here was over the bureau's proposal to interconnect the Columbia river power system with the Central Valley project in California. NWPPA considered this an attempt to subsidize irrigation districts at the expense of the power user in the Northwest. But for the most part the goal of the association is a constructive one—to help build up the groups that are its members.

One of the proud names in the Northwest is the Inland Empire, which is in the state of Washington between the Bitterroot range of the Rocky Mountains and the Cascades to the westward. It is one of the most beautiful regions in America. Stretching from sky to sky like a huge checkerboard are great wheat fields, in spring green and brown, in fall yellow and gold. When the wheat is harvested in September, the fields of stubble look as if a giant had run his fingers through a golden nap. Poplar trees and stands of ponderosa pine are the only break in an endless horizon of wheat. The Inland Empire Rural Electrification Association is, as one might expect, one of the most flourishing co-ops in the country.

Most of the members are wheat farmers whose average gross income in these years of prosperity has been $60,000 a year. Many of the members are commuter farmers. That is, they live in small country towns and commute out to their wheat fields. That is true of Dan Hopkins, a founder and president of the Inland Empire co-op. Hopkins lives in the town of St. John, where he has a handsome glass and brick ranch house to which he returns at dusk, hot and grimy from the day's work in the fields.

Inland Empire has some 3000 miles of line serving more than 5000 members. That the co-op has prospered is not surprising when it is realized that many members own farms as large as 2500 acres and use up to 20,000 kw-h a year. They come closer to being small industrialists than farmers, managing a highly mechanical production job with machine shops on individual farms that are better equipped than most small town repair shops. High usage has enabled the co-operative not only to pay back its debt to the government on time but in addition to make a sizable advance payment as a cushion for any bad years in the future.

The manager of Inland Empire is Ted Waller. A native Hoosier, Waller came to the state of Washington as a railroad telegrapher after World War I. He took a degree at a Washington college and then taught school for fifteen years before joining the co-op. An expert accountant, he was once drafted by REA to teach other cooperative personnel the intricacies of bookkeeping.

Before Waller assumed management of Inland Empire, there was discontent among the co-operative's members. The management was not too efficient. The relationship with the members had been neglected. One of Waller's first acts as manager was to hire Robert Smith, a young man working with the Bonneville Power Administration, to take over public relations. Waller himself set out to tighten up management. A meter-testing laboratory was installed and testing equipment and engineering services provided while at the same time purchasing and replacement methods were systematized.

Public relations being at a low point, Smith's job was more difficult. He published a monthly newspaper to keep members informed of what was happening in their co-op. He spoke at Grange meetings throughout the co-op's territory and explained its purpose and methods to businessmen at Rotary clubs and Chamber of Commerce meetings. He has worked up an elaborate pictorial presentation to be shown at state and county fairs. A most effective leaflet has been put out explaining the achievements of the co-op answering questions raised by critics. "Does the co-operative pay taxes?" is one of the questions raised. And the leaflet gives the following answer:

"Yes, it pays every tax that any other electric utility in the state of Washington pays, with the exception of federal income tax. Because it is a nonprofit organization, there is no profit on which to pay income tax. Since the co-operative was organized, it has paid over a quarter of a million dollars in taxes directly to county, state, and federal treasuries, plus many hidden taxes such as excise and gasoline taxes included in the cost of materials purchased."

As with almost everything else in the Northwest, the dominant element is low-cost power and the availability of that power. Inland Empire is supplied by the Bonneville Power Administration, which markets the energy from all the Columbia River dams. The co-op picks up its power at nine different delivery points from the Bonneville transmission network. This has meant a great saving in transformers and substations and lines that would have under other circumstances been overloaded and consequently rebuilt. "Even the Washington Water Power Company is willing to wheel Bonneville's power for us," says Waller with a smile. "And why not? They receive two kilowatts from the Bonneville Administration for every kilowatt they deliver to Inland."

Power costs the Inland consumer about half what it would in other states. The minimum bill for Inland is $1.80 and for any use over 300 kw-h a month the farmer pays about three fourths of a cent a kw-h.

This cheap rate has made it possible for farmers of the Inland Empire to experiment with electrical house heating. Waller qualifies as an expert in this field. For two years he conducted a test in co-operation with the Bonneville administration. His house was equipped with electrical heaters and a maze of meters and recording instruments. "Every day for two years I read those meters," he recalls, "and if you don't think that was some job, you're crazy." If the cost of power can be kept low enough, Waller believes that electrical space heating can compete with heating by oil provided the houses are well insulated. Convinced by Waller's experiment of its practicality, today 250 Inland co-op members are heating their homes with electricity.

In the fall of 1951 Inland Empire co-operators held an open house day to celebrate moving into their new office building in Spokane. Looking back over the years since the co-op was founded in 1937, they could be proud of what they had built through their own enterprise. With its lines touching ten counties and serving five thousand families, the co-operative had grown until it needed a permanent home. Through a loan from REA of $210,000, the largest ever made for this purpose, this office had been built. To mark the day the co-op directors sent this message to all members:

"Now that the lines have been extended to nearly everyone who wants service, the days of hoping someday to have electricity for our members is over. The wish has become a reality and the transition symbolized by the structure that is now the permanent home of your co-operative. As a member of the co-operative you are part of an organization that performed the impossible and brought a new life to farm people in your community. That's why your co-op is a whole lot more than just an outfit that sells electricity."

The Lincoln Electric Co-operative, Inc., of Davenport, which is a neighbor of Inland Empire, claims the highest average use in the country—800 kw-h a month. Many bills run as high as a thousand.

In spite of the low-cost power—the rate of Davenport is 1.34 cents per kw-h—rising costs are beginning to be felt. The Davenport co-op was temporarily compelled to go into its maintenance reserve with a prospect that rates would be raised. Line foremen who in 1934 were getting $125 a month with no overtime, in 1951 drew $432.60 a month and time and a half for overtime. Materials have correspondingly soared in price.

In Oregon the public power movement has been somewhat retarded by the conservatism of the state. When legislation was passed permitting the formation of Peoples Utility Districts, a provision was included in the law requiring that the voters decide in each instance on major acquisitions of the property of private power companies and on bond issues. Sponsored by the private utilities, this provision crippled the PUDs in Oregon. But the co-operatives have done well.

The Dalles, Oregon, is the home of the Wasco Electric Co-operative. On the Columbia River, the town got its name from a French word meaning trough or deep chasm in the rocks. In the early days of the Northwest The Dalles was a transshipment point on the voyage down-river. Lewis and Clark stopped there on their trip down the Columbia. And John Jacob Astor and the Hudson's Bay Company sent their trappers through the town.

The first farms in the region had been on the creek bottoms out through the high plateau overlooking the town. Along Five Mile, Eight Mile, and Fifteen Mile creeks are rich orchards which produce apples and sweet cherries. On the plateau above The Dalles the volcanic ash soil is ideal for wheat. Where the land is thin and dry, sheep and cattle graze on the June grass. Here, too, is one of the largest stands of virgin timber left in Oregon.

In 1940 most of this rich farming country had no electricity. The Pacific Power and Light Company ran its power lines from town to town. But the company, like most private utilities throughout the country, wanted a large cash payment to hook up farms lying back from the main road.

One rancher who lived in Wasco County near The Dalles was Eric Johnson, a Swede who came to America with his family in 1906. They came to Oregon because they had a relative working in the big timber. Eric Johnson became a wheat and cattle farmer. From his ranch he could see the power company lines less than a quarter of a mile from his house. But when he asked Pacific Power and Light to hook him up, he was told that the 11,000-volt line was too big to tap for such a small load.

Sixteen of his neighbors had been told the same thing by the company. They decided to hold a meeting to see what could be done about getting their own electricity. In a local restaurant they discussed the possibility of a Peoples Utility District or an REA co-op. Gus Solomon, an attorney who has since become a federal judge, told them how they could form a co-operative through which they could obtain a loan from the Rural Electrification Administration in Washington. That was in April of 1940. By June the farmers had hired an engineer to map out their co-op's system. In August the REA had granted the Wasco Electric Co-operative a loan. Six months later the new organization was ready to energize its first twenty-six miles of line.

A celebration lasting for a week preceded the day the juice was turned on. The climax was a huge picnic. Several hundred farmers from all over Wasco County had gathered with their families to watch the final ceremony. First the sheriff of The Dalles and a mounted posse gave a drill. Then came speeches by Grange officials, who had done a great deal to help carry out the project. They heard, as thousands upon thousands of other farmers have heard at similar gatherings all over the country, how through co-operative effort they had done what the private companies said was impossible. When Emory Davis, president of the Wasco co-op, took a long stick and tripped the energizing switch, a great cheer went up from the crowd.

Since that spring day in 1941 the co-operative has grown steadily. Lines have spread gradually around the towns of Dufur, Wamic, Maupin, Morrow, and Grass Valley. The co-op's network has grown to a thousand miles serving 1350 farmers. The man who has managed the Wasco co-op through these years is the same Eric Johnson who was told by the company that his ranch was too small to serve. Johnson now rents his place and lives in town to be near the undertaking into which he has put so much of himself. A big rugged man with a gruff yet friendly manner, Johnson is the moving spirit in the co-operative. He is more than an efficient manager. He is active in the whole public power program of the Northwest and has several times come to Washington, D.C., to testify before committees of Congress on the need for pressing the rapid development of the Columbia River. Reflecting the intense regional consciousness of the Northwest, Johnson frequently asserts the independence of the Wasco co-op. He has taken the REA symbol off the co-op building because he believes that it is important to foster the understanding that this enterprise is self-liquidating, self-owned, self-managed, and taxpaying. "There's no grant or subsidy in this company," he often says. "Why should we have an REA sign on our co-op office?" he asks. "After all, I don't write the name of The Dalles Bank on my ranch if they happen to hold my mortgage."

Johnson believes this same self-assertion within the NRECA has made it the strong organization it is. An admirer of Clyde Ellis, he relates how Ellis once came to the Northwest to find out why the national association wasn't gaining more members. Johnson and other Northwest power leaders told Ellis the direction in NRECA must come from the bottom up and not from the top down. "Clyde listened to us," says Johnson, "and took our advice. Since then our national association has reflected real grass-roots feeling."

Almost complete area coverage has been achieved by the Wasco co-operative. In one section of the county there are only seven farmhouses in twenty-nine miles, but a perlite mine was brought into operation in this section and today is using $20,000 worth of power a year. That made it possible for the co-op to pick up those seven widely separated farms. Several other large users of electricity, lumber mills, and small manufacturers, have helped make it possible to serve the thinnest lines.

Johnson believes the members understand and appreciate Wasco's policy of area coverage. Immediately after World War II farmers in adjacent Sherman County were faced with choosing between whether the co-op or the Pacific Power and Light Company would serve them. A big meeting was held to hear proposals from both parties. After the 165 farmers assembled heard the offer of the private utility, Eric Johnson arose to make his proposal. He pointed to his maps of the area hanging on the wall and then he said to the company's representative, "All right, if you will promise to serve everybody on this map as we do, we'll give you our maps and let you serve the farmers." The spokesman for the company declined and the Wasco co-op was extended into Sherman County.

Power use has gone steadily up in the two counties. New ranch houses are being equipped with every sort of electrical device. On the bottom land, fruit growers are utilizing some 1200 horsepower for orchard irrigation. Aluminum pipes that can be easily shifted are used to spray the trees with water, thereby increasing the yield of cherry and apple orchards.

The mounting demand for horsepower poses the chief problem for Manager Johnson. The Bonneville Power Administration which supplies power to the Wasco co-op, is scraping the bottom of the power barrel. A Wasco member using 70 kw-h in 1941 is today using some 800 kw-h a month. Co-op lines which were designed for what was once an optimistic load of 125 kw-h must be "heavied up." "It makes me damn mad to hear people talking about the completion of rural electrification," says Johnson, "as though we could just sit here for thirty-five years when our lines would fall down. A company, co-ops included, must add to and improve its plant each year. With contractors asking $1800 to build a mile of line, we will continue to need REA loans."

In 1951 the Wasco co-op built a new office building in The Dalles. To make way for the low concrete and glass structure on a quiet shaded street, more reminiscent of New England than Oregon, it was necessary to tear down a large Victorian house that had once been the home of a wealthy banker. The change seemed to symbolize the new era. In an editorial entitled "For whom the bell tolls" a local paper wrote: "An empire is crumbling. Its achievements are as outdated as the pony express. Its watchwords have lost meaning. . . . As the bell tolls out the old, a brave new world arises and new prospects for democracy in action."

With ninety-four out of every hundred farms in the Northwest electrified, the job is now to heavy up the co-ops and PUD systems and to pick up the remaining pockets still without electricity. One such pocket was in and around the town of Moulson, Washington, situated in the extreme northern part of the state a few miles from the Canadian border. Part of the frontier only fifty years ago, the town is today the farthest outpost of rural power expansion.

The visitor to the community of Moulson-Chesaw in the fall of 1951 would have felt an air of expectancy. Leaving the rich orchards of the Okanogan Valley and driving up into the hills, he would have seen electric power poles standing without wire. In the farmyards were other poles ready to be used. Most of the houses had already been wired and farm families were waiting to energize their lines. This was the end of a twelve-year struggle to get electric power, a struggle that had encompassed every possible disappointment.

For years the Moulson community had tried to get the private power company to serve them. But the Washington Water Power Company saw little reason to extend its lines into the hills. Located in the saddle of a hill, the village consisted mostly of a brick schoolhouse, a general store, a post office, and some gray weatherbeaten houses. It was not much of a customer. When the grain elevator burned down, the railroad tore up its track and after that the village began to seem like a deserted mining town.

Farm leaders did not, however, lose hope of getting electricity. By 1939 the county agent and a local attorney had interested Moulson in the REA program, which at that time, under the dynamic leadership of John Carmody, was helping farmers everywhere to build their own lines. At a community meeting it was decided to form the Moulson-Chesaw Co-operative. Jess Smith, a wheat farmer, was elected president. Like so many others in this rapidly growing region, Smith is not a native. He and his wife came over the mountains from Idaho in a model-T Ford. Before he became a farmer he was a bookkeeper for the local elevator company. With his friendly smile he had got to know almost everyone in that whole part of the country and he was a natural choice for president.

But the co-op had scarcely been incorporated when war-time restrictions put a stop to all plans. By the end of the war the voters of Okanogan County, in which Moulson is located, had voted to establish a public utility district. They also voted to buy up the Washington Water Power Company's facilities located in their county. Once again farm families hoped to receive electric service. In 1945 REA approved a loan for the PUD so they could extend service in the Moulson area. But the utility district turned the loan down for several reasons. The REA applied its customary restrictions in the way in which the funds could be used. For one thing, it declined to permit some obsolete equipment to be used in the area financed with the federal loan. At about the same time the PUD had manager trouble, which disrupted plans for rural service. Then in 1948 a flood destroyed a large part of the PUD lines, creating a difficult financial situation.

The result was that after three years of negotiation the PUD told

Moulson farmers that they would extend electric service at a minimum rate of eleven dollars a month on a ten-year guarantee. Before the offer could be accepted, the PUD found it necessary to ask in addition a cash contribution of $765 from each prospective customer-member. This stirred up a lot of indignation. "We helped to vote the PUD into existence," said Moulson farmers, "and now what is the difference between a utility district and a private utility?" Charles Hortz, the Moulson postmaster, said, "Well, some of us could afford to pay that $765. But the lady who lives just across the road from me, she couldn't, and that means she'd have to go without service." So in 1949 they turned back to REA.

The small system the Moulson farmers proposed to build looked barely feasible. On 157 miles of line there were only 150 customers. Moreover, the country around Moulson is mountainous, which means expensive construction. REA was doubtful about the loan at first. But by this time Ray Dart, a member of the local Grange's Power Committee, had become active in the organization of the co-op, and all obstacles went down before his persistence. Dart enlisted the help of his congressman, Walter Horan, and Horan expedited negotiations with the REA. The REA agent in Spokane, Guy Keffer, negotiated a favorable contract with the Bonneville Power Administration. A wheeling agreement was worked out with the Okanogan County PUD so that power will be delivered to the co-op at three and one half mills. Also under this arrangement the PUD will maintain the co-op's lines. Eventually, to get the benefit of joint management, it may be necessary to merge with the PUD. But through the co-operation of the utility district, the federal government, and, above all, the farmers themselves, electricity has at last been brought to this small community that is smack up against the Canadian border. It has been co-operation in the true meaning of the word.

Although low-cost power was perhaps the major factor in bringing electricity to Northwest farms, sheer dogged perseverance was almost as important. One of the persevering farmers bound to get electricity for his own farmstead and the farms of his neighbors is Olaf Rise. Born in Norway, he emigrated to America with his father and mother, who settled down to farm in Northwest Washington. Olaf and his five brothers are typical of the many Scandinavian families who brought with them a long tradition of co-operative and public ownership. Today the Rise family is one of the largest landholders in the Moulson district. A tall, rangy man with the high coloring of the Scandinavian, Olaf is shy and soft-spoken. But beneath this exterior lies an understanding of and a fierce belief in the rural electrification program. Anyone who tells him that rural electrification was inevitable and that the private companies would have done it in any event will find an argument. "Except for the pressure of

REA's program," he says, "the farmers today would still be sitting in the dark listening to promises. Like anything else," Rise adds, "the power business needs competition and our co-ops have supplied that competition."

The transformation that has taken place in the Northwest in twenty years is remarkable. A whole new way of life has come into being. And this is true even though only ten per cent of the major hydroelectric projects on the Columbia and the Snake have been constructed. The changes that can come in another twenty years can be even greater if the program is pushed nearer to completion, as almost everyone in the Northwest intends that it shall be.

IN NO DEPARTMENT of politics are there more complications, more pitfalls, more "on the other hands" and "yes, buts," than over the issue of electric power. REA is a part of the federal power program. While it is in many respects separate and independent, it has to an increasing degree in recent years become involved in the dispute that has developed around the low-cost power generated at the large federal hydroelectric projects either built or being built. That was perhaps inevitable, since the REA co-operatives, after the initial phase of construction, have become concerned over alternative sources of power which would free them from complete dependence on private suppliers, and they have also been more and more determined to obtain low-cost current from the federal projects in accord with the law which makes them a "preference" user.

In the political year of 1952 that was the root of the matter. The original REA act provided that the co-ops could borrow money to build their own generating systems and transmission lines. Under the policy developed through the years first in Congress and then in REA such loans have been made where it could be clearly demonstrated that either no other source of power was available or where the power could be generated at a lower rate than that offered by any private supplier. In a half-dozen states since the end of the war applications for generating loans have been directly related to the availability of hydroelectric power from federal dams. Steam plants are essential to firm up the hydro power if co-operatives are to get the benefit spelled out in the Flood Control Act of 1944.

These applications have become the center of the attack by the private utilities. This is the focus of the dispute—the benefits of low-cost federal power, if necessary to be made available through the construction by the co-ops of steam-generating plants and transmission lines—which promises to play a part in our political life for a long time to come. In Congress, in the courts, before state legislatures and state utility commissions, through public appeal the industry is doing everything possible to limit the REA program to the distribution of power obtained almost entirely from private suppliers or at any rate over their lines and on terms fixed by them.

Very few members of Congress criticize REA directly. There are exceptions, of course, such as Representative John Taber of New York, who includes REA within the wide embrace of his economy drive. Taber has again and again called for reduction of REA appropriations, insisting that the program was so nearly complete as to require little or no further financing.

Most critics, however, are less frank. They belong to the "yes, but" school. In the periodic hearings to which REA is subjected, Administrator Wickard is frequently confronted with interrogation along the lines used by Representative Harold Cooley of North Carolina, chairman of the House Agriculture Committee in May, 1951. He begins by stating that he supported the REA program long before Wickard took office and that he is interested in seeing that the co-ops have low-cost power. "But at the same time," he quickly adds, "I am anxious for them to use existing facilities." He then wants to know whether the administrator is trying to take over the power companies in their entirety. "Do you," he asks, "sit as judge and jury on applications for a generating and transmission loan? Do you intend to go into competition with private industry?" Cooley went further to say:

"I do not think anybody on this committee—certainly I would not—would want to do anything that was going to delay the delivery of power to the farmers of this country. At the same time, I do not want to do anything to impair the financial security of existing companies that now are adequately furnishing service. . . . I do not think REA was created to go into competition with private industry. I think it was created to furnish electric light and power to the areas of this country where private industry has refused to do so. . . . I do not think it was created with the idea of getting the cheapest possible rate to the consumers in the rural areas. That was not the original idea, because the whole thing was predicated on high costs of production."

It developed in these hearings that Cooley's concern was over plans of North Carolina co-ops to construct their own steam plant and transmission lines tying in with the Buggs Island federal power dam. Two events seem to have given the matter special importance insofar as Cooley was concerned. First, the House had just turned down a Department of Interior request for funds for transmission lines to carry power from Buggs Island, including one into North Carolina. This line, if built, would have enabled a few municipalities and electric co-ops in that state to get abundant, low-cost power from Buggs Island. Cooley quoted one of the North Carolina co-ops as stating that they themselves would build the transmission lines to make the power available to North Carolina farmers. Such a loan, Cooley intimated, would be circumventing the will of Congress.

The second event that apparently lurked in the background was the then current struggle of the Old Dominion Electric Co-operative in the neighboring state of Virginia. Old Dominion, formed by co-ops in Virginia, had received an REA loan of $16,000,000 to build a steam plant and 1100 miles of transmission lines as a link with the Buggs Island dam. In other words, Virginia was doing what North Carolina co-ops were planning to do in order to get the benefit of low-cost water power.

In the Buggs Island controversy are all the elements of the struggle being waged in so many areas and on so many fronts. The Virginia Electric and Power Company has shown great resourcefulness in blocking the steam plant and the transmission lines. When the application for the loan was first made, the co-ops were paying about one cent per kw-h to VEPCO for their power. The company had previously testified before the Federal Power Commission that they could not sell for less and that in fact that rate represented a subsidy, because the power actually cost more to produce.

Yet at the strategic moment when the Old Dominion co-op had petitioned the State Corporation Commission for approval of the loan from REA, the company reduced the rate to 7½ mills. Witnesses for the company testified that the offer was made with the specific purpose of killing the loan. And the commission responded by doing just that.

The company's next move was to offer to sign a five-year contract at the new low rate. But that would have tied up the co-ops just in the period when Buggs Island power was coming in, beginning in 1952. A long and complicated dispute over wheeling charges followed, with the co-ops convinced that the rate asked by the company, in spite of an ostensible reduction, was unreasonable. That was the position, too, of the Southeastern Power Administration. The company has already succeeded in killing a government-built transmission line from Buggs Island to the important and rapidly growing aeronautical research center at Langley Field. After long and wasteful haggling, the upshot was a one-year contract at the 7½ mill rate, which is for both sides at most a temporary expedient.

On the basis of his voting record Cooley is friendly to the REA program. The record compiled by the National Rural Electric Cooperative Association shows him as having voted twenty-four times in favor of REA measures and six times against. This record is typical of most of the members of the agriculture committee who come from rural districts where such votes are closely watched. The strength of organized farmers behind the program is still formidable.

But the evidence is growing that this strength is not so great as it was and that it is being tested at every point with the view to a frontal attack. A subcommittee of the House committee on expenditures in the executive branch of the government, headed by Representative Porter Hardy of Virginia, looked into REA in 1950. Hardy, who has a reputation for being fair-minded, appeared to be strongly biased against REA, and the impression given was of a search for scandal.

The Hardy committee found the major area of conflict to center on loans made to federations of co-operatives which in turn entered into agreements with power administration agencies of the Department of Interior. It is on these "super co-operatives," the industry calls them, that the attack of the utilities is concentrated. Yet the report issued by the Hardy Committee was comparatively innocuous. Following a course calculated to offend almost no one, it recommended further study of congressional intent with respect to generation and transmission loans and particularly where federal hydroelectric projects were concerned. The committee found that the co-ops, when well managed, served the interests of the American taxpayer satisfactorily. The report criticized some accounting and auditing procedures and pointed out that of the 991 REA borrowers, 247, or twenty-five per cent, operate at a book loss. REA experts explain that this does not necessarily reflect on operating personnel, since in the early stages of operation losses are anticipated and REA lines are on the average only six years old.

When, and if, the fight over generating loans comes to a climax in Congress, an important factor will be the attitude of representatives from urban areas. They come mostly from districts served solely by private power companies. Those companies find ways of contributing, and often generously, to campaign funds. Liberal congressmen will sometimes admit that on the power issue they take a much milder line than they would like to, in fear of reprisal.

In this struggle the power companies have great resources which they seem willing to spend freely. Now and then the extent of those resources is publicly revealed. The House committee investigating lobbying, under the chairmanship of Representative Frank Buchanan of Pennsylvania, late in 1950 issued a 520-page report showing in detail the large sums spent on Washington influence by 179 corporations, many of them utilities. Besides the money spent for advertising and Washington representation, many had contributed to such organizations as the National Tax Equality Association, the American Enterprise Association, and America's Future, Inc., which spread virulent and often highly distorted propaganda. In addition they had contributed to two hate-mongering groups, the Committee for Constitutional Government and the Constitutional Education League.

Such companies listed large sums. Thus the Pacific Gas and Electric Company reported spending more than $300,000 in the previous three years. The Georgia Power and Light Company listed expenditures of more than $175,000. Influence spending by the Virginia Electric and Power Company added up to nearly $40,000. The Carolina Power and Light Company of North Carolina was down for $230,000 during three years and five months. Pennsylvania Power and Light Company listed spending of more than $140,000 over the same period.

The utilities have some loyal friends in Congress. The voting record of Representative Richard Wigglesworth of Massachusetts shows that he voted thirty-seven times against REA and never for any REA measure. Representative Joseph Martin, minority leader in the House, has a record of twenty-three negative votes and one affirmative. Congressmen from Massachusetts need have no fear of reprisal from farmer members of electric co-operatives, since the State Utility Commission in 1937 prohibited REA co-ops. Rhode Island and Connecticut likewise have no rural electric co-ops and the program has been weak in New York.

The political strength of rural electrification in Congress is in the loyalty of tried and tested friends who have consistently supported it in season and out. Outstanding among Republicans in the Senate is George Aiken of Vermont. Speaking to Missouri farmers in the summer of 1951, Aiken let go a slashing attack on the private utilities for their attempt to claim credit, through the promotion of a rural electrification week, for the job that had been done. He denounced the industry for blocking the efforts of farmers in the initial phase to get power for themselves. Other Republican senators actively behind the REA program are William Langer and Milton Young of North Dakota, Wayne Morse of Oregon, and Charles Tobey of New Hampshire.

On the Democratic side in the Senate many of REA's staunchest supporters are from the South. High on the list are Lister Hill of Alabama and Lyndon Johnson of Texas. Paul Douglas of Illinois and Guy Gillette of Iowa have been loyal friends. Following the resignation of Harry Slattery, Gillette was mentioned as a possible REA administrator. Warren Magnuson of Washington, and Richard Russell of Georgia have supported the farm power program on most measures in which it was at issue.

In the House the division tends to be on party lines. John Rankin of Mississippi has voted for REA thirty-six times, just one short on the aye side of the record set by Wigglesworth of Massachusetts on the nay side. Clarence Cannon of Missouri, chairman of the House Appropriations Committee, has been a stout friend in that strategic position. So have Mel Price of Illinois, Henry Jackson of Washington, and, unfailingly, Bob Poage of Texas. A consistent Republican supporter has been Merlin Hull of Wisconsin.

In 1952 as in 1948, the development and distribution of electric power promises to be a campaign issue. Although many of us missed its significance at the time, President Truman's farm speech at Dexter, Iowa, in 1948 was the key to his campaign and perhaps as well the key to his victory. To a huge crowd of farmers who had come from miles around in their big shiny new cars Truman recited the farm benefits flowing from the New Deal and the Fair Deal, including rural electrification. Then he slammed into the Republicans as the party of Wall Street, asking the farmers whether they wanted to lose all that they had gained. The pundits from Washington wrote this down as bad politics on the theory that farmers in Cadillacs were no longer interested in the "menace" of Wall Street. But Truman proved that he knew what he was doing and the final count showed that the votes of farmers weighed more heavily in his re-election than those of any other group.

Governor Thomas E. Dewey in his farm speech at Des Moines a little later in the campaign was so cautious as to draw only a lukewarm response. In a speech in mid-October at St. Paul he vigorously endorsed the REA program, telling his audience that the Republicans then in control of Congress had "voted by far the largest amount ever provided by any Congress to speed electricity to our farms—$800,000,000." But he made no reference to any controversial phase, such as the generating and transmission loans.

In his campaign looking to the Republican presidential nomination Senator Robert A. Taft of Ohio has done a thorough, careful organization job appealing to major groups of voters, with the farmer in the No. 1 position. As a matter of fact, long before he began even a pre-convention build-up Taft had tailored his approach to the mass of America's farmers. During his senatorial campaign in 1950 he had sponsored legislation providing federal loans to farmers to build co-operatively owned grain elevators. That undoubtedly helped to explain why he carried every rural county in Ohio except two, receiving in some farm counties as high as seventy-seven per cent of the total vote cast.

As regards rural electrification, Robert Taft must be considered a "Johnny-come-lately." His apparent acceptance today of some generation and transmission loans to co-ops is a radical shift from a position once noted for its record of votes against the rural power program.

In late September of 1951 he spoke at the dedication of a new steam plant of the Minnkota Power Co-operative at Grand Forks, North Dakota. As Dewey had done three years earlier, he boasted of the record of the Republican 80th Congress in appropriating more money for REA "than all previous appropriations put together and that it breathed life into the program from which you are now reaping the benefit." Then Taft went on to say:

"It is true that in the case of the REA the money to establish these facilities, which in the power field are very expensive, has been loaned by the Government. But that should not change the co-operative character of REA. So the government also subsidized the first transcontinental railroads and other enterprises where, for one reason or another, private capital could not undertake the complete support of new and risky development. . . . A true co-operative is just as much private enterprise as a private utility. . . ."

Mr. Republican went on to endorse the principle of co-operatives as representing the collective bargaining power of farmers as labor unions represent the collective demand for the workers. By implication he endorsed the right of a co-operative to build generating facilities where power at a fair price was not available. But this was not enough to suit the more radical Republicans in a state where the Non-Partisan League has from time to time been the dominant factor in politics. There was grumbling, too, over Taft's attack on farm subsidies and the support program. At the same time criticism came from the extreme right, with an association of Minnesota businessmen taking a full page in Minneapolis papers to condemn Taft for his stand in the Senate Finance Committee against applying drastic taxation to co-ops.

But whatever the words spoken by either side in the course of a hotly contested political campaign, the effort to block REA co-ops from sources of low-cost power produced by federal dams went on unceasingly. In Federal District Court in Washington ten Missouri power companies filed suit against Secretary of the Treasury Snyder, Secretary of the Interior Oscar Chapman, Secretary of Agriculture Charles Brannan, REA Administrator Claude Wickard, and Douglas Wright, administrator of the Southwestern Power Administration. The suit sought to enjoin them from granting loans to the Central Electric Power Co-operative and the Northwest Electric Power Co-operative to build steam-generating plants and transmission lines.

Here was the familiar issue once again. Missouri co-operative officials hoped through the steam plants, which would firm up hydro power, and the transmission lines to obtain current from SPA's dams. They came to Washington to testify to the urgent need for more power. H. M. Zaricor of Sikeston, Missouri, said that his co-op had experienced 113 power failures in 1949. The executives of private utilities in the region took just the opposite stand, arguing that there was sufficient power and that the co-ops could obtain it from private suppliers at a lower rate than they could through the proposed tie-up with SPA.

Utility spokesmen cited figures of the Federal Power Commission showing a twenty-eight-per-cent reserve supply of power in the Southwest. The commission holds that fifteen per cent is sufficient for reliable service. The co-operators from Missouri replied that while this might be shown to exist theoretically over the whole area, they knew from actual day-to-day experience of shortages that repeatedly handicapped Missouri farmers.

In their attack utility executives made much of the fact that the power to be produced by the steam plants in conjunction with SPA's hydro power would be in excess of what the co-ops themselves could use. Quite apart from any other factors, perfectly valid engineering reasons exist why this should inevitably be so. To send electricity over long distances high voltage is essential, and this necessitates building lines with carrying capacity in excess of present co-op requirements. To make this feasible, the co-operatives would lease their transmission lines to SPA, which would also buy all the power from the co-op steam plants, selling the excess over and above co-op needs to municipalities and private utilities. The whole purpose of this exchange would be to enable the co-ops to buy firmed up hydro power at a lower cost than if it were entirely generated by steam.

The utilities insist on regarding the co-operatives as merely an arm of Government. Here, they say, is one agency of Government that will pay a profit to another agency of Government. This ignores, of course, what even so conservative a Republican as Senator Taft points out—namely, that the co-operative is itself private enterprise. "REA is building a larger plant than it needs," said Warren Porter of the Kansas City Light and Power Company, ". . . and there is not a single privately owned utility in the United States which can survive against such competition." REA lawyers in briefs defending the exchange agreement with SPA said:

". . . There is no competitive intent. Any excess capacity of the lines would be to supply municipalities already owning their own facilities or to private power companies. . . The facilities are in effect dedicated to REA to use except for the surplus capacity considered above for a period of forty years. . . If the purpose of the loan is to make service available to unserved persons in rural areas, that purpose would not appear to be altered merely because one of the incidental beneficiaries is another agency of the Government. . . ."

The National Rural Electric Co-operative Association denounced the suit brought by the companies as a propaganda stunt. Clyde Ellis pointed out that since Congress had heard the complaints of the utilities and had taken no action on them, and since the loans had been granted under law, it was fairly clear that the companies did not actually hope to win their suit. He also pointed out that private power companies enter into exactly the same arrangement with SPA and other federal agencies as the co-ops propose to do.

The Government first asked that the suit filed against the three cabinet officers, Wickard and Wright be dismissed. This was denied and later the case was set down for argument. In a campaign year such a lawsuit is likely to get inextricably mixed up with the campaign oratory. Eventually it will in all probability go to the Supreme Court. This could mean a delay of not less than three years from late 1950 when the suit was first filed.

As World War II had done, the rearmament drive brought scarcities of copper, aluminum, and the other materials that go into power facilities. It also meant grave shortages of power in various parts of the country. James F. Fairman, head of the Defense Electric

Power Administration in the Department of the Interior, told the Maryland Utilities Association that the outlook for 1952 was more serious than it had been at any time during the war that ended in 1945. He estimated that the increase in the power load from 1950-53 would be greater than the total power load developed in the United States in the entire fifty-seven years' history of the industry before World War II; that in the Southeast the relationship between power supply and demand would be critical in the winter of 1952-53. In the industrial North Central region it became necessary to interrupt steel production because of power shortages. And the brown-out in the Northwest was news throughout the nation.

With the scramble for scarce materials co-operative leaders were fearful the utilities would see to it that rural electrification got what was left over if, indeed, it got that much. When Clifford McManus was appointed administrator of defense power in the Department of the Interior, they were deeply suspicious. As president of the Georgia Power Company, he was considered a utilities man. He chose Fairman, out of the Consolidated Edison Company of New York, as his deputy. The big utilities, it was feared, would run the show their own way, with the co-ops and the municipalities scarcely getting a look in.

The first big contest came over the allocation of scarce materials. McManus proposed that his office have the authority to pass on the allocations to individual co-ops. Co-op leaders were indignant at this proposal. They were perfectly willing to accept whatever was their fair share of the total amount of copper and aluminum assigned to construction of lines and generators. But they wanted the right to say how this should be used among the co-operatives. Both Wickard and Ellis made strong representations to Secretary Chapman. They pointed out that while it was proposed that the power administration should control individual allocations to the co-ops, the industry was asking for the right to make its own assignments from its share of scarce materials. What was fair for one should obviously be fair for the other. After the dispute had gone on for some time Fairman, acting in the absence of McManus, granted the co-ops through the REA the right to do their own allocating.

McManus resigned not long afterward and Fairman was made administrator. He has shown a much more understanding attitude toward the problems of rural power users. In a speech in the fall of 1951 he said:

"The truth is that electric power is one of the fastest growing ingredients in our economy. The facts are readily ascertainable. In the period from 1946-50 the total kilowatt-hours for residential and rural use in this country increased seventy-three per cent—a tremendous gain in four years. All of the devices for electric living in the home are still readily available as a matter of national policy, so this increase continues at an accelerated pace. The expectation is that approximately 1,800,000 residential customers will be added in 1952. In the last five years the kilowatt-hours used on the farms of this country have increased 160 per cent. Farmers have been asked to increase their total production. With the draft and defense jobs pulling man power away from the farms, rural electrification and the substitution of power equipment must be provided if the food goals are to be met. Curiously enough, some people who accept the necessity for the manufacture of more farm machinery take a dim view of rural electrification."

In the Northwest the problem of power supply was so acute that the great gains of the war and the postwar years seemed threatened. Representative Jackson of Washington was pushing in Congress a bill to authorize $60,000,000 for eight steam-generating plants which would become part of the Bonneville distributing system, firming up hydro power from the Columbia River. Three would be large plants of 100,000 kw-h capacity each. The other five would be smaller generating turbines of a maximum of 20,000 kw-h each. This steam capacity would be integrated into the Bonneville system at the extremities in order to offset line loss.

No direct opposition was coming from the utilities in the region. Their managers may have felt that the net effect would be to make available to them even more low-cost power at Bonneville's postage-stamp rate. In Portland the Portland General Electric Company obtains about two thirds of its power supply at the lowest rate in the country, and this, along with the city's rapid expansion, helps to explain why the company is making more profits than ever before. The opposition came from the Chamber of Commerce and other groups that have consistently opposed the development of federal water power projects.

The Atomic Energy Commission, as Jackson was well aware, since he is a member of the joint Senate-House Atomic Energy Committee, was about to increase by 200 per cent its entire operation. This would mean enormous new demands for power at both Oak Ridge in Tennessee and the Hanford plant in Washington. A huge new plant was going up at Paducah, Kentucky, and the Tennessee Valley Authority was unable to supply any of its power requirements. This was part of the strength of America, and a vital part, called into being by the threat of Communist aggression.

That strength was not alone in vast industrial plants producing the fantastic new weapons about which President Truman boasted. It was on America's farms, where food productivity was increasing under the spur of new demands, and where the new hand, the magic hand of electricity, was making these increases possible. In the larger sense the power issue is not confined to Washington nor even to the state legislatures and the utility commissions.

This is a truth of which co-operative leaders have become increasingly aware. They realize that the political decision will be made by the men and women out in the country who have gone a long way toward achieving for themselves one of the great advances of modern life. If they take this achievement for granted, if they regard their co-operative as only another utility, then they are likely to lose their independence and with it the benefits of low-cost power.

The Very Reverend Francis B. Sayre, Jr., of the Washington Cathedral, in an address at the 1951 annual meeting of a southern co-operative, aptly expressed the democratic basis of co-operatives. Pointing out how broad the co-operative principle is, including in its scope the church itself, he stressed the importance of each member and of his awareness of his own responsibility for the common good of all; that this is the larger meaning of co-operation and the significance of its achievement. That significance is far broader than the material gains of light and power. These material gains are in a sense an end in themselves. But in as much as they free men from drudgery and toil, they are means to the leisure that can bring wider horizons, understanding, knowledge, conviction, the faith in God and the goodness of man that are at the base of a free society.

Chapter Twelve

FOR THE FUTURE

THE propaganda of the private power industry has recently
been devoted to convincing the public that the job of bringing electricity to the farm is finished. The theme of the costly and clever
campaign is that the whole undertaking can now be wrapped up and
put on the shelf as something that is past and done. Actually, if one
considered the potentialities of this marvelous new force in the
hands of the farmer, it has only begun. What we have seen so far is
the establishment of a base from which growth can continue in a
pattern far more startling than the cycle of change that has occurred thus far.

In several of his books, notably *Malabar Farm*, Louis Bromfield
has suggested what this pattern might be. While industry has been
moving toward mass production and efficiency through the
assembly line, giving industrial workers the highest standard of living in history, Bromfield points out that until quite recently
"agriculture has been moving in the opposite direction toward lower
and lower production per acre, per man hour and per dollar invested." Farm production must be increased by modern methods,
and in achieving this end electricity may be the greatest aid since
the introduction of Eli Whitney's cotton gin.

Agriculture is, of course, the great power-consuming industry of
modern society. The farmer uses more power to do his work than
any other industry except transportation. The factories of the
United States, for instance, consume only half as much power as do
the farms. It follows that the farmer must necessarily search for a
cheap form of power. In this search he has utilized the wind,
animals, falling water, gasoline motors, and the human back. In the
past fifteen years the American farmer has had the miracle of electric power. This fluid energy is cheaper, more efficient to use, and
more pliable than any of the other forms of energy.

But the age of electric agriculture lies ahead. At present electricity in farm production is largely limited to time-consuming chores,
although intensive experiments are being carried on to apply it to all
fields of agriculture. The farmer himself, an innate conservative,
has only begun to comprehend what electric power can mean in his
work.

A variety of uses have been found for the electric motor which
turns, lifts, pumps, heats, freezes, grinds, and sharpens. But this is
still, in a sense, a primitive use of electricity. The infinite
possibilities of electro-chemical agriculture are only just beginning to be explored. The potentialities of irrigation with electric

pumps in areas where irrigation has never been contemplated suggest greatly increased crop yields. The irrigation of pastures in the Midwest, where rainfall is comparatively well balanced and distributed, may seem superfluous. But Bromfield produced on his pastures in Ohio in a summer of normal rainfall nearly half again as much grass by irrigation. Electric pumps delivering a thousand gallons of water a minute onto the ground enable one man to irrigate nearly twenty acres of pasture and meadow.

Electricity may evenutally enable the farmer to process much of his produce right on the farm. If with the help of electric power he can perform some of the basic processing jobs, he can get higher prices for his crops. He can reduce spoilage en route to market. And he may be able to reduce the huge toll taken by rodents, weevils, mold, and fire that proper handling by new methods can largely eliminate.

Farmer Logan of Morrow County, Ohio, used to take his dusty potatoes to market as soon as he had harvested the crop. Others would process them and move them on to the wholesale distributor. Several years ago Logan decided that he could process the crop himself and thereby get a higher price for it. Farmer Logan set up an electric conveyor belt to carry his potatoes through automatic scrubbers. When they were scrubbed clean they were dried with a set of electric lamps. Then the crop was sorted and packaged and stored in sheds until top market prices prevailed. Logan found that the higher prices he received paid for the processing machine in one year of operation.

Another farmer, John Feisely, suffered losses from soft corn spoilage. Feisely's son thought the spoilage could be stopped by storing the corn in cribs where it could be dried with large six-bladed electric fans. Still soft, the new crop was placed in corncribs and the fans turned on. In the first experiment spoilage was reduced to zero.

Tobacco farmers have long been plagued with the slow process of curing tobacco to obtain the bright lemon-colored leaf that the market desires. The commonest method of curing up to the present time has been to use wood and sawdust in fires that must be stoked continuously for several days. Many growers have experimented with automatic electric controls on tobacco curers. In Virginia farmers were losing part of their multimillion-dollar crop between the cutting, grading, and curing of the tobacco and its sale. Through better grading, hardier plants, supplemental irrigation, and better curing practices Virginia's tobacco growers may increase their annual income as much as $18,000,000.

Hay as well as tobacco can be cured or dried with electricity. Farmers living in areas of plentiful rainfall east of Kansas City found, after experiments made in the Tennessee Valley, that they were able to reduce the spoilage from rain, and produce better hay through barn drying with electric fans. The hay can be cut and lifted into the barn after only a few hours in the field. Electric fans can there dry it with far less nutritive loss than if dried by the sun. This same process is proving successful even in states west of Kansas City, where the intense sun quickly dries the hay left in the field. Many farmers are turning their fans on grain crops which are often shattered by field curing.

Likewise peach growers in Arkansas are using electrically operated sprayers, conveyors, graders, and defuzzers to pack and market a top grade of peach which pays off in higher prices. In Pennsylvania an apple grower, Charles Packard of Blair County, has used electricity extensively in his five-hundred-acre orchard. He has eleven miles of pipe line, powered by electricity, to spray every tree in the five hundred acres of his orchard. When the fruit is picked, Packard places the apples in a cold-storage plant large enough to hold the bulk of his crop. In this way he is able to release his crop on the market gradually.

The dairy farmer of today is absolutely dependent upon electricity. The electric milkers, water pumps, water heaters, and refrigeration are indispensable to the farmer wishing to produce Grade-A milk. Milk is taken from the cow electrically; it is processed and stored properly with the aid of electric machines.

The poultry farmer, like the dairy farmer, finds it increasingly difficult to compete without the extensive use of electric power. Electric incubators hatch the eggs. Electric brooders keep the young chicks warm. As the birds grow older, their water is pumped and warmed by electricity. Chicken houses are ventilated by electric fans. And the electric lamp is even used to wake them up earlier in the winter months of short daylight. Chickens sleep when it is dark, but when the lights in the chicken houses are automatically turned on in the early winter morning, the fowls are waked up and lay more eggs. If the chickens are raised to sell as poultry, electricity enables the farmer to process them right on his farm. Scalding water prepares the feathers for picking. Pickers and waxers complete the process, and finally the farm freezer enables the farmer to keep the dressed poultry on his farm until the market price is right, or until he can conveniently take his dressed fowls to market.

The economics of the electric motor applied to farm work are simple. The electric motor allows the farmer to apply a small amount of power to a task for a long period of time instead of using a large amount of power for a short time. Thereby it helps reduce the peaks of farm labor. The one-horsepower motor can do as much work in one hour as the average man can do in a day. And this power costs so little. For four or five cents a farmer can pump a thousand gallons of water from his well. For those few cents he can milk thirty cows, or heat five gallons of water, or shell thirty bushels of corn, cool ten gallons of milk, or cut one ton of silage and raise it thirty feet into a silo. No longer is the farmer tied to a large machine expensive to operate, unwieldy to apply to a job, and too large for the work to be done. With an electric machine small enough for his job, the small farmer can close the gap of efficiency between himself and the large factory farm.

The farmer has been slow to substitute electric power for other forms of animate and inanimate power. As one agricultural economist, Joe Davis, has written, "Electricity seeps rather than surges into the farm organization." The average farmer is inclined to be skeptical about any innovation in agriculture. A farmer will install lights in his house. Then he may buy an iron or radio, perhaps next a refrigerator. Later may come a milking machine, pig brooders, shop tools, and so on, until electricity has spread into every phase of farm life. As would be expected, prosperous farmers use more electricity than do low-income farmers. Davis believes that the high price of equipment may be a greater factor than the cost of electric power in limiting the use of electricity on the farm.

There are many agencies helping the farmer to find new uses for electricity. The known uses for electric power in farming now number some four hundred, and the end is nowhere in sight. Many state colleges are engaged in research work, as are the large utility companies and the Department of Agriculture. At the federal Government's agricultural research station in Maryland, engineers are trying different methods of freezing produce such as apples and vegetables. Electricity is being used experimentally to control bacteria. Fluorescence is used to sort and compare eggs, potatoes, corn, and other produce. Radiant heat is used in chicken houses to control dampness and disease, to stimulate fowls sexually, and also to dehydrate vegetables and to dry cotton, rice, and sweet potatoes. Electrical traps have been used to kill insects such as the European corn borer which caused great damage to corn growing in the field. A Pennsylvania engineer, John Nichols, has studied irradiation of the soil. "It is an almost breathtaking conception," he writes, "The irradiation of the soil by high frequency during plowing, resulting in possible eradication of grubs, mites, and insect eggs, could provide an environment for crops to grow in free of any blight or pest." The benefits of electricity to agricultural production are still largely for the future. Scarcely touched upon, the field lies wide open for experiment and development.

Future experiment and development must take more into account the peculiar character of electric energy. If the farmer has been sceptical of this new energy, agricultural scientists and technicians have been slow to realize the change in modes of farming that electricity calls for. The electric motor up until now has largely been adopted to power old machinery and to lighten old work procedures.

Farm educators still think in terms of the big machine and hand labor. Indicative of this thinking was the Department of Agriculture's massive work, *Science in Farming*. Published in 1947, this book records in detail large field machinery, chemicals, and crop practices that the present-day farmer has at his command. But there is not a single reference to the small electric motor and its role on the farm!

Professor F. W. Duffee, chairman of the Department of Industrial Engineering of the University of Wisconsin, in an address to the Edison Electric Institute at Denver reported on studies showing that "farm electrification is still in the very early stages of development." He estimated that not more than twenty-five per cent of the connected load on the farm is represented by farm electrification equipment. The rest is in lights and household appliances. The figure for 1938 was only ten to twelve per cent.

Duffee reported on experiments made on the Wisconsin Electric Research Farm, established at the university with funds supplied by the Wisconsin Utilities Association. These experiments have shown the need to redesign the farmstead in order to make the most efficient use of electricity. Thus cow trainers, electrically operated devices to train cows to keep their stalls clean, work much better in longer stalls. "Dairy barns may be planned somewhat narrower when a barn cleaner and narrow center alley are used," Duffee said. Similarly the hog house must be redesigned to get the utmost out of electric power. Average annual consumption on Wisconsin farms in 1950, Duffee pointed out, was about 4000 kilowatt-hours. Consumption on the Electric Research Farm was 44,800 hours, or eleven times as much.

The greatest change thus far has been worked on the farmhouse and farm living, and that is as it should be, for it has helped to minimize the migration away from the farms that set in half a century ago. Secretary of Agriculture Charles Brannan said in 1950 that the very crux of the problem facing American agriculture in the years immediately ahead is the steady drain of farm workers into industry. The contrasts between life on the farm and life in the city were so great that inevitably the younger generation, in an era in which traditions were being shattered, was drawn to the easier life of the towns. The Science Advisory Board found in 1935 that hard living conditions were largely responsible for the decline of farming as a way of life.

Many observers, among them Harcourt Morgan of TVA, Charles Collier of the Georgia Power Company, and Charles Kellogg of the United States Soil Survey, have deplored the loss by rural states of the wealth of young people who after their upbringing and education migrate to industrial states. Again there were, and are, many reasons for the exodus, among the most important being the fact that the youth of this century, unlike their forefathers, are unwilling to remain, in the Biblical phrase, "hewers of wood and drawers of water." The advent of rural electrification in Georgia, Charles Collier believes, has slowed this rural migration from a run to a walk. Running water, refrigeration, oil furnaces with electric air blowers, the radio, and now the advent of television have in a short fifteen years revolutionized farm life. As Vincent Nicholson, a pioneer of rural electrification, told Congress several years ago, "In this short period of time we have literally bridged the gap between the Middle Ages and the twentieth century."

Although the great majority of farms today have electric light, a radio, a washing machine and an iron, much remains to be done. In a country that prides itself on the marvels of its plumbing, only a third of the nation's farmhouses today have inside bathrooms. In the not too distant future, air-conditioning units to cool the sleeping rooms of the farmer and his family and thus to temper the fierce summers of the Midwest and Southwest should not be uncommon. If it improves their health and efficiency, then it will also increase production and enlarge the common good. Such a suggestion would have seemed highly fanciful twenty years ago, but not today. Incidentally, the development of a cheaper, standardized conditioner would seem to open a new field of industry—for private industry.

The modernization of the farmhouse is essential if future generations are to be willing to stay on the land to produce America's and the world's food. Claude Wickard recently told Congress, "I know that I would not be able to get my daughter and her husband to take over the management of my farm if these modern conveniences did not at least in some measure compensate for the long hours of farm work. I also know that we would have a lot more trouble in getting hired help on the farm to keep up production. We are having to compete with manufacturers of television and automobile parts for the available labor of the community. We are paying comparable wages, but I do not think that would attract the kind of help we must have if we do not have electricity and running water in the tenant houses."

Modernization of the farmhouses, together with the expanding use of electricity in agricultural production, makes clear the future of the Rural Electrification Administration. The geometric rate of increase in the use of electricity on the farms has already created the need to heavy up lines built ten or fifteen years ago. This is equivalent to building four-lane highways where a two-lane road once sufficed. For the use of electricity on the farms has surpassed even what REA engineers in 1935 optimistically hoped it might be. When the program was on the drafting boards fifteen years ago, private utility companies called Morris Cooke's engineers starry-eyed dreamers because they predicted that the farmer might use sixty kilowatt-hours of electricity a month. Rural electrification was a social, not an economic program, said the utility company executives.

Today the average amount of power used by the American farmer is double the estimate of 1935. And the latest survey by the Department of Agriculture indicates that farms electrified for fifteen years even now double their use of power every five years.

Rebuilding the rural lines to carry heavier loads has been undertaken by commercial companies and REA co-ops in the past several years. The cost of heavying up the systems will equal or even exceed the original cost of the REA lines, since prices for essential materials have nearly doubled. Some co-operatives will be able to finance their own rebuilding, while others will have to borrow further from REA. Harlow Person, consulting economist to REA, believes that despite the expense of heavying up, the co-operatives will be able to carry the added financial burden since the use of electricity has increased so greatly. Person says that although census figures show over three fourths of the farms electrified, the work of rephasing is not more than half done.

The farmers themselves have found it necessary to heavy up the wiring of their farmhouses and barns. The Edison Electric Institute has urged farmers to plan for the future loads they will expect to put on their system. Indicating the growth of electricity on the farm, the Institute says, "Important as it [house wiring] is, the careful planning of exterior wiring and service equipment is of even greater importance. In 1930 a two-wire, 60-ampere service was considered adequate for most farms, even in dairy regions. Today the development of new equipment has reached the point where some farmers are finding a 100-ampere service inadequate." Government engineers point out that heavying up the lines without interrupting the flow of current to the farms is a real problem. For power failure, which to the city dweller is at most an inconvenience, can cost the farmer heavy losses in spoiled produce.

Reconstruction of REA-financed systems is not the only problem facing the co-ops and the REA administrator today. Area coverage is important—the job of electrifying the "thin" areas of America's farmland. The core of the problem is a strip of states—Montana, North and South Dakota, Nebraska, Kansas, and Oklahoma—which lie nearly in the center of the country. There are few farmhouses and little rural industry in the far reaches of this Great Plains country and the economy of Great Plains farming is uncertain. Large areas are faced with prolonged drought. Some five million people were driven off the land by the drought which ended in 1935. The high cost of power and the great distance between farmhouses make it hard for a co-operative to operate successfully.

Ten years ago it was assumed that Congress would have to subsidize the construction of lines into this country if electricity was to be brought to the Great Plains farms and ranches. But the coming of the Missouri Valley hydroelectric development with the potentialities for cheap power and irrigation, and in the tremendous growth in the use of electricity on the farm have changed the picture. Already power from the huge federal dam at Fort Peck in Montana is flowing to fourteen co-operatives in the Dakotas and to virtually all of the co-operatives in Montana. This power, which costs about half what fuel-generated power formerly cost, will allow these co-ops to add some twenty-five thousand members to their lines in the next ten years.

Typical of what can happen in this underdeveloped country can be shown in the Death Valley region of California. Death Valley is one of the most thinly populated areas in America. Heretofore a co-operative project would not have been practical. Today, however, a large corporation is interested in mining in Death Valley. The appearance of rural industry and the possibility of irrigation in nearby areas are at last making an REA co-op a possibility.

Certainly the completion of rural electrification in the Great Plains states will depend in large measure upon the continuing support of the well-organized and outspoken Farmers' Union. With several thousand local chapters in the Dakotas, Colorado, Montana, and Oklahoma, the union is in a strong position to aid its five hundred thousand members in electrifying their farms.

The Farmers' Union today has espoused the generation and transmission policy of the most militant co-ops. This position, which is more advanced than that of the American Farm Bureau Federation or the National Grange, is taken for two prime reasons. First, the Farmers' Union is an active champion of the family farm and the little farmer. The union well recognizes that without electric power this small farmer cannot compete today against the large factory farm. Secondly, the instability of Great Plains farming tends to make that region's farmer more radical in his approach to his problems. And in the future few problems will have greater importance to him than a dependable and low-cost supply of electric power.

Outside of the Great Plains area, REA faces the job of completing area coverage within a single state. In many areas, for instance, there are unelectrified pockets within a commercial company's territory. The farmers in these pockets are too few in number to support an electric co-op. Their only hope for service lies in the competitive pressure to expand created by nearby co-operatives. Altogether it is estimated that there are approximately a million farms still to be served with electricity. That is a large order for the future.

Mississippi poses another kind of obstacle to complete rural electrification. The most predominantly rural state in the South, Mississippi has the South's lowest percentage of electrified farms.

Among the factors working to hinder rural electrification are illiteracy, a high percentage of tenancy, and sharecroppers. These factors and racial taboos against Negroes, who comprise half the state's population, make for a miserably low farm income. Co-operatives find that many farmers cannot afford the fifty dollars it costs to wire their houses.

The cost of power in Mississippi has been high, and power contracts between the co-ops and their wholesale suppliers have contained clauses that have hindered the development of rural industries. But Wickard reported recently that "power companies have reduced their rates considerably, especially after consideration was given to a generation and transmission installation in that area."

But those two words, generation and transmission, are the focus of a dispute on which the whole future of the electrification program may turn. Thus far 165 borrowers have had loans for generating plants and seven for transmission lines only. In recent years the opposition of the utility industry has centered on this phase of the program.

The conflict over the right to generate and transmit electricity is related to the controversy over the appropriation of federal funds for hydroelectric projects and how the power from such projects will be dispensed.

The utilities are quite willing to buy power at the low rate charged by the Government, taking it as it comes off the bus bar and integrating it in their own system. In fact, the utility industry today gets a far larger share of this low-cost power from federally built dams than do the co-ops. To the extent that they can buy this power at a low price and sell it at a higher price, retaining a virtual monopoly of federal power, the utilities have no objection to the subsidies they claim are inherent in government dams. Co-operative leaders fear that unless they can build their own feeder systems to these federal dams eventually they will be compelled to pay a much higher rate for this current, the chief benefit thus going in profit to the power companies.

A possible compromise is suggested in the pattern established in some areas. In 1949 a federation of co-ops at Bismarck, North Dakota, received a loan to build a generating unit, substations, and transmission lines to tie in the co-ops with the Fort Peck Dam in Montana and at the same time with the Montana-Dakota Utilities Company. Under a contract approved by REA in Washington, Montana-Dakota Utilities arranged for the construction of the generating unit and other facilities and now operates them for the co-ops. Taking power from Fort Peck, the company integrates it into its own system and delivers the desired number of kilowatts to the co-op load center. For this power delivered by the company the co-ops pay the

Bureau of Reclamation that operates Fort Peck. As a result of this arrangement, according to Cecil Smith, president of Montana-Dakota Utilities, "the Bureau of Reclamation, the REA, and our company have brought about one of the quickest and most widespread developments of REA anywhere in the country."

In other parts of the United States and especially in the Southeast, in Virginia, South Carolina, North Carolina and Alabama, and in the Southwest, the power companies have in instance after instance refused to work with the co-ops. Co-operative leaders feel that they do not bargain faithfully; that any contract will later be revoked by the state utility commissions. Power company presidents from the Southwest have regularly appeared before Congress to argue against the REA program. They have fought the co-ops before state commissions and they have raided co-op territory. These companies have been largely responsible for the propaganda battle denouncing the co-ops as socialistic or communistic. Now the co-ops in federation—the Brazos River generating co-op in Texas is an example—are powerful enough to build transmission lines directly to the source of low-cost hydroelectric power. In some cases this fact alone has brought a remarkable transformation of the attitude taken by the companies.

The drive will undoubtedly continue to strike out of the REA Act the right to make generating and transmission loans. The reader has seen that Chairman Harold D. Cooley of the powerful House Committee on Agriculture regards such loans as "taxpayers' loans going into a program in competition with private industry." Great pressures are being put on state legislatures and state utility commissions to curb the program. Friends of REA in Congress say that if it were not for NRECA, the generating and transmission phase would long since have been stricken out.

One of REA's staunchest supporters over a long period, Bob Poage of Texas, calls the right to generate a "birch rod in the cupboard" to compel power companies to offer reasonable rates. "You have but one bargaining power with the power companies," Poage has told the co-ops, "and that is the ability to provide competition. There is not any other bargaining power that you have. . . ."

There is one man who will determine how this issue is finally decided. That is the farmer back on the farm. If he becomes indifferent and takes for granted the achievement thus far, then the opportunity will be at hand to destroy the birch rod. Other users of electric power will get the preference, as they did before 1936, and the almost certain prospect will be for a rise, gradual at first but more rapid later on, in the cost of power on America's farms. If that happens, we are not likely to see further and even more remarkable transformations that electricity can work, both in the home and in the field, to widen horizons not only of the farmer but the city dweller who will benefit from larger and richer harvests.

Chapter Thirteen
DEMOCRACY AT WORK

THE license plates on the cars outside the inn told the story. The directors of the National Rural Electric Co-operative Association were holding their summer meeting at a lodge near Stowe in the Green Mountains of Vermont. Most of the states were represented—Texas, Maryland, Ohio, Illinois, Georgia, Missouri. The members from the Far West had come by plane or train. But most of the men on the board had used the family car in the accepted American fashion which makes a journey of a thousand or fifteen hundred miles almost as casual a matter as was a visit to the next-door neighbor in another day.

For two days, from nine in the morning until late in the afternoon, the board sat around long tables in what is in the winter a skier's recreation hall and reviewed the progress of electrification on the farm as carried out by some nine hundred co-operatives. This was a pretty good cross section of America. These men, chosen by their respective statewide organizations to serve on the national board, are leaders in their own communities and their own states. Here is democracy at work, a group of individuals who have assumed the responsibility of providing for themselves one of the basic elements of modern life.

There is pride in this and a sense of the concentrated work that has gone into it. The meeting is friendly and good-humored. Tom Craddock of Texas, secretary-treasurer, asks for enough time to brush up his minutes. And from the chuckle that runs around the room you know that this is a long-standing joke. In his round, genial person Craddock seems to radiate good will. Regional differences stand out strongly. You could never mistake Mike Bennett as coming from anywhere but Arizona. And P. J. Donnelly has in him something of the bigness of North Dakota. Maury McWilliams of Alabama speaks with the easy voice and mellow accent of the South.

Year after year these men have worked together, some of them since the founding of NRECA. The board functions in the careful framework of organization headed by Clyde Ellis, executive manager of the association. Before each member is a folder containing the agenda of the meeting and the proper memoranda for each item on the agenda. A great many matters must be settled and the discussion is almost always more prolonged than had been foreseen.

If this meeting in the troubled summer of 1951 had any central theme, it was where the co-operatives would get an adequate supply of low-cost power. Again and again the question came up in relation to one subject or another. In the background of the discussion was the concern these men felt over the utility industry's propaganda attack against the co-operatives. How to meet this attack the board was not quite certain, but they knew that the time had come when they had to meet it.

The issue came up when the board considered whether or not to make a rebate out of accumulated surplus to the co-operatives belonging to the national organization. A rebate of two hundred thousand dollars would have been possible. But several directors pointed to the need for a fund with which to combat the attack of the private utilities. Bill Roberts, NRECA's editor and information director, outlined a proposal for a nationwide radio program which would help to get the facts before the public. An outsider could not help but reflect on how small these sums were in relation to a propaganda battle with the giant utilities. Yet in earnestness of intention and persistence of purpose, these men may make up in large part for the slick, highly paid public-relations techniques that well-heeled commercial industry can employ.

All was not sweetness and harmony at this board of directors meeting. It would have been surprising if so many rugged individualists from every part of America all thought alike on every subject. One of the most warmly debated subjects was the relationship between the rural electric movement and the American Farm Bureau Federation. Many of the directors have close ties with the Farm Bureau both in their respective states and on the national level.

One of these men is Donnelly from Grafton, North Dakota. The Donnelly family are of Scottish descent, and have been prominent in North Dakota agriculture as raisers of shorthorn cattle. A prosperous, conservative rancher who has been active in Farm Bureau work, Donnelly reported on the meeting of a special committee of the Farm Bureau to consider both sides of the private versus public power controversy. The private utilities had sent a battery of experts to that meeting, including Purcell Smith, principal spokesman for the power lobby in Washington. Donnelly had undertaken to present the viewpoint of the co-operatives in need of low-cost hydroelectric power from federally financed projects. But as he told the other directors, "I didn't know enough. The next time I meet them I am going to be prepared so that I can answer back. I'll have all the facts and figures."

This led to a general discussion of the attitude of the national leadership of the Farm Bureau and whether or not it was actually on the side of the private utilities. There were some sharp exchanges. Peppery H. C. Knappenberger of Arkansas, who is a prosperous rice planter with numerous other interests in and around Blytheville, declared it as his opinion that the Farm Bureau was no different from the National Association of Manufacturers. This drew a protest from Harold Whitman of Illinois, who said it was necessary to remember that the Farm Bureau was a large national organization and that it contained members who held many viewpoints. Consequently its position on highly controversial subjects could not please everyone.

But invariably the board came back to that thorny problem of an adequate power supply. They heard Ellis warn that the propaganda drive of the power companies against the co-operatives is now showing up in state and national legislatures. This was confirmed by individual members who reported that in state after state laws favorable to co-operative enterprise were in jeopardy. Ellis talked about the provisions in federal law that gave preference to public agencies and co-operatives for the purchase of hydro power generated at federal dam sites. Despite this preference, the co-ops have been able to get less than four per cent of this power, the rest going mainly to private power companies and to industry. "We must stress our right to this power as written into law," says Ellis, "and we must try to build the transmission lines that will link us directly with this low-cost power if we are going to meet the growing demand of our members for electricity."

Ellis's warning was underscored by board members from those states where the struggle to get federal power has been sharpest. Both Jack Needy of Missouri and J. E. Smith of Virginia reported on tactics used to shut off their co-operatives from sources of federal power. And both Needy and Smith warned that whatever happened to them would sooner or later happen to the rest.

Clyde Seybold of Indiana called for caution, telling his fellow directors to be careful not to infringe on the capital investment of private enterprise. Clyde is tall, austere-looking, inclined to the conservative side. He is a Master Farmer of Indiana, the prosperous owner of a corn and hog farm near Rockville. For twenty-five years Clyde has been active in the Farm Bureau and for fifteen years in the Rockville Rural Electric Membership Co-operative.

From Gordon Loveless of Vermont came a proposal for a conference including all those concerned with public power looking to a constructive solution of what should be the power policy of America.

Toward the end of the session, Walter Harrison of Georgia submitted the report of a special power committee. In the voice that comes out of his big frame like thunder, Harrison affirmed a basic desire to be independent. "We don't," he said, "want to take any customers away from any private utility. We just want to be independent." The report proposed that a consulting engineer be hired to put all the facts before Congress and the public. This was a note which had been struck from time to time throughout the meeting—how the friends of REA in Congress were too often without the facts while the opposition rushed up with complete details supplied by public-relations experts for the private power industry. The board then discussed where the next summer meeting should be held. South Dakota, Colorado, Oregon, and Washington all wanted it. This decision was left up to the officers and executive committee.

To the visitor, Vermont seemed an ideal setting for this democratic undertaking; Vermont, where the roots of an older democracy still live in the town meeting. In many respects Gordon Loveless serves as a kind of bridge between the older democracy and this new development which is a translation into the power age of those earlier forms. Canadian-born, Loveless came from Ontario Province, where he had seen an earlier experiment in rural electrification under Sir Adam Beck. Loveless's frank, friendly personality soon won him friends, among them Vermont's senior Senator George Aiken. Personnel director for the state of Vermont, Loveless gives a good part of his free time to co-operative endeavor. He has served as a director of the Vermont Co-op Council and the Co-operative League of the USA. Without any cant or pretension, he simply believes in people and what they can do when they work together.

One of the first things that Gordon Loveless noticed when he came to Vermont in 1931 was the high cost of power. High power costs today still restrict the growth of electric co-operatives in Vermont. The power companies in the state depend largely upon the New England Electric System for their power and are charged a rate set by this concern. That rate is high, and so is the farmer's bill. The result is that electrification has been slow in developing Vermont's farms.

The need for Vermont and for all New England to develop hydroelectric sources has been pointed out recently by a committee studying New England's economy. Hydroelectric development would help the region to reduce the cost of electric current which at one and a half cents a kilowatt-hour is one of the highest in the United States. How to break through this situation for the time being at least seems to have co-operative leaders stopped. They point to the weakness of Vermont's Public Service Commission and the wiles and influence of the private power lobby in Montpelier.

As the board members left to go their separate ways the feeling was strong of ties once more affirmed; of a union strengthened by a common resolve, a shared responsibility. These men, most of them, interrupted urgent day-to-day jobs for this board meeting. Elton Trowbridge of Wyoming, a tall, slender plainsman, said, "I left just as they were about to put up seven hundred tons of alfalfa. I shouldn't have left, but I had to come to this meeting." Trowbridge is a schoolteacher turned rancher. He has a real conviction in his job as president of his co-operative. When he leaves the national meeting, Trowbridge, like the other directors, must attend regional and state meetings and finally the annual meeting of his co-operative. This organization reaches far down below the obvious surface into every corner of rural America.

That is its strength and it is at the same time one of the most important phases of the whole program. The physical transformation worked by power on the farm is abundantly evident. To anyone who looks at the evidence objectively, it is clear that this transformation would not have happened without REA working through the co-operatives, that is to say, with the farmers themselves. The degree of competition brought about by the co-operatives in their drive for low-cost power has profoundly influenced the price of electricity. This influence has spread far beyond the confines of the rural power field. But important as this is, and it seems to me hard to exaggerate its importance, the achievement in terms of leadership is almost as significant. So much in American life today comes on order out of the controls exercised by big business in New York or the controls exercised by big bureaucracy in Washington. Millions of Americans have lost a sense of participation in their own destiny. Here are Americans, just plain American citizens, who have done a big job for themselves. They did it when the rich and the powerful said condescendingly, disdainfully, that it could not be done.

It has called forth at every level leadership of an exceptional quality. The potentiality was always there. It remained only for the challenge to bring it out. It seems to me one of the healthiest pheonomena of our times, the reversal of the growing trend toward dependence on the bigness generated out of those two capitals on the eastern seaboard.

The significance of this new growth of democracy is above all in the self interest that it develops and sustains through each community and in the nation as a whole. The directors of NRECA who met in Vermont were for the most part working farmers. But they are also leaders in their respective communities. Harry Nuttle is president of the bank at Denton, Maryland. Walter Harrison is editor of the newspaper in Millen, Georgia. Raymond Huck is Master of the Waterford, Ohio, Grange. Harold Whitman is active in the Farm Bureau at Cameron, Illinois. Russell Anderson, until he became an active leader in rural electric circles, was a banker in Ogallala, Nebraska. As these men wrestle with problems of power supply, taxation, and management, they become aware of how their co-operatives fit into the regional and national framework. They understand the need of making themselves heard in the state legislatures and at Washington. And, what is most important, they are determined to be heard.

We Americans are always looking for the ultimate formula, the final panacea that will solve all of our problems. No one would claim that electrifying America's farms has done that. While it has greatly increased farm production and raised the standard of life of farmers everywhere, it has tended to accentuate certain long-range difficulties confronting the nation. Thus the greatly increased use of electrical pumps for irrigation in the Southwest has caused the water table to drop at an alarming rate, raising in more acute form the issue of the perilous balance between land and water resources.

But the important thing is that this great far-reaching program has shown once again that Americans, in spite of the prophets of gloom, know how to solve their problems, how to roll up their sleeves and pitch in and do what has long needed to be done. It is the equivalent in the age of power of the quilting bee and the barn-raising, and it is every bit as American in concept and in practice.

Yesterday Today and Tomorrow

Chapter Fourteen
THE FIGHT FOR SURVIVAL

THE early years of the rural electrification revolution as the initial volume shows were a record of dedicated idealism, of stern effort and unflagging determination to correct an injustice long ignored. It was a part of Franklin Roosevelt's New Deal and one of the most successful undertakings of that adventurous time. But there was a marked difference in that the Rural Electrification Administration from its inception in 1935 was largely self-sustaining. It was true that a low interest rate to link areas with widely scattered hookups was in effect a subsidy. But resolute down-to-earth farmers and ranchers were the strong central core that meant the loans were repaid with virtually no default.

It seems incredible today that at the start of REA only ten per cent of rural America was electrified. Farmers and their wives were hewers of wood and drawers of water in ways that had changed little over the centuries. In the vanguard in Congress for REA were leaders like George Norris of Nebraska, George Aiken of Vermont and Sam Rayburn of Texas who can never be forgotten as the founding fathers of a great national movement. Those first two strenuous decades were the solid base on which the progress of the following years has been built.

The growth that has come about since 1952 is amazing. It can be measured by money; loans today in the billions rather than the millions of that earlier time. In so many bold and innovative ways electric co-ops have moved into new fields and relationships. While there are regional patterns, it is a national movement building on the resourcefulness and energy of hundreds of thousands of co-operators. An extensive literature has grown up reflecting the pride of these co-operators in their accomplishments.

Important is the contribution the rural electrics have made to America's total energy supply in the generating and transmission co-ops that have come into being. While it is small, from four to four-and-a-half per cent of the total volume of electricity produced in America, it represents an addition in areas where it was most needed and the present deficit would be that much greater without it. Furthermore, new generating plants are being built by co-ops and will go on line when every additional kilowatt counts. The most significant fact is that today 99 per cent of rural America is electrified. At the same time the demand for power is increasing at a geometric rate as farmers turn to new uses for electricity in the production of food and fiber, one of America's greatest assets is the standard of living here at home and in trade overseas. This expanding demand is the reason a greatly expanded REA program is essential.

While the growth has been phenomenal, a dramatic incident occurred that threatened at one point to put a stop to the entire program. The way the attempted sentence of execution was met is one of the exciting chapters in the ongoing struggle of the co-ops to continue to improve their rightful place in the American economy. More abrupt, it was nevertheless reminiscent of the early years when investor owned utilities sought to checkmate the REA movement or at the very least to keep it within bounds set by the utilities themselves.

On December 29, 1972, the REA direct loan program was wiped out and with it the telephone loan program. This was done, incredible as it seems in retrospect, by a press release issued by the Department of Agriculture. While it had been authorized by Secretary of Agriculture Earl Butz, he had obviously acted as later events were to show on orders from President Richard Nixon who had just been re-elected in a landslide carrying every state except one. What made it more extraordinary was that during the campaign, administration spokesmen had boasted of the record loans made during the previous four Nixon years. Butz himself had made filmed statements for co-op regional meetings on the President's behalf.

This abrupt action by the administration was in some ways a blessing in disguise for it served to demonstrate the political power of the National Rural Electric Cooperative Association. With director members representing 46 states, statewide organizations highly organized, NRECA is one of the most pervasive self-generating organizations in the nation.

As NRECA's executive vice president and general manager, Robert D. Partridge's first move was to call on Butz and REA administrator David A. Hamil to ask what the blow meant. He was puzzled by a reference in the press release to a substitute loan program under the Rural Development Act. What did it signify? Was it a means that co-ops, some in immediate need of loans to recover from damaging winter ice storms, could count on as they had relied over the years on REA?

Partridge found that Butz and Hamil were in the embarrassing position of being unable to supply any details about the substitute program. It was not ready for operation, and until policies and procedures could be worked out no loans would be available. REA had come to a full stop. In his editorial column in *Rural Electrification*, NRECA's monthly magazine, Partridge wrote:

"With all due respect for the administration's right to make policy judgments, I must candidly say that I do not think it is wise policy to hamstring the ability of rural electric systems to meet expanding needs and adequately serve their consumers in the face of a mounting energy crisis. That is not the kind of energy policy we need. . . This is the most critical challenge that we have faced in the history of the program. . . ."

The next step was for Partridge along with all the staff of NRECA's headquarters in Washington to carry the case to friends of the rural co-ops in Congress. And those friends on key committees were legion. It was, however, the following step that dramatized the grass roots base of NRECA. At Partridge's invitation co-op leaders throughout the country were called to Washington to a rally to show Congress the extent of the support for restoring the REA program. They came 1400 strong to fill the ballroom of the Mayflower Hotel on January 23 and 24 and listen to speaker after speaker tell the farmers and ranchers of the righteousness of their cause.

One of the most fiery and impassioned speakers was Sen. Hubert Humphrey of Minnesota. While this was before the onset of the cancer that ended his long and eventful career, he was in bed with a touch of the flu and a fever of 103° when asked to speak at the rally. He would appear, he said, but could stay for only a few minutes. Speaking without a note, and unfortunately his words were not recorded, it was characteristic Humphrey weighted with the American past and charged with the politics of his populist Minnesota background. Calling up the memory of the embattled farmers of the Revolutionary War at Lexington and Concord, he went on:

"You embattled farmers can do in the year 1973 for free government, representative government, what others almost 200 years before have done. . .You can use this program, the REA program, as a test of the legitimacy of government. You can use what has been done to demonstrate whether or not one man, by executive order, can ignore the will of the American people through the Congress assembled. You can determine for once and all whether or not a President can continue to impound funds that have been appropriated by Congress."

Humphrey's speech, that with his enthusiasm went on for more than an hour, drew repeated whoops and hollers such as the Mayflower ballroom had seldom heard. Rally participants were fired up to invade Capitol Hill and carry to members of Senate and House the case for restoring REA. They were calling for action on the Humphrey-Aiken bill in the Senate and the measure advanced by Frank E. Denholm of South Dakota and Bob Poage of Texas in the House with many co-sponsors. Effective lobbyists, they were given an unintended assist by President Nixon.

At a press conference at the end of January Nixon was asked about the two per cent rate for REA loans. He began by saying he had always supported REA because he used to represent the 12th district in California which was primarily agricultural with orange groves. Although, he went on, it had been largely subdivided he continued to vote for REA because of his origins. He continued:

"But what I have found is that when I first voted for REA, 80 per cent of the loans went for the purpose of rural development and getting electricity to the farms. Now 80 per cent of this two per cent money goes for country clubs and dilettantes, for example, and others who can afford living in the country. I am not for two per cent money for people who can afford five per cent or seven per cent."

In an exchange with Butz before a Senate agricultural committee hearing, Sen. George McGovern refuted Nixon's statement with statistics provided by NRECA. They showed that while in Congress Nixon had voted 13 times out of 16 against rural electrification issues. In an appearance on NBC's Today Show, Hubert Humphrey expressed his scorn over the dilettante remark. If Nixon had thought the program was for the benefit of dilettantes, Humphrey demanded, why hadn't he exercised his veto last year rather than relying on executive fiat to kill the program?

In testifying before the agriculture committee along with a host of witnesses supporting the Humphrey-Aiken bill, Partridge said that REA was a program for business, industry, residents, farmers, all people in rural areas who need central station electric service. It was essential to develop rural areas and relieve the pressure on overburdened cities. He had previously pointed out that no loan can be made to a country club or any entity other than by a bona fide rural power system. Expansion of the cities into outlying farm land was an obvious reason why an increasing percentage of non-farm families were hookups on co-op lines.

By a vote of 317 to 92 the House on April 4 passed the Denholm bill. It provided for insured and guaranteed loans, most of the former to be made at a standard rate of five per cent interest with a special rate of two per cent for rural electric systems meeting certain criteria such as coverage of areas with consumers averaging only two or three to the mile. Use of the funds authorized by Congress was to be mandatory. Constricting amendments were repeatedly voted down. The Senate had already passed the Humphrey-Aiken bill by a vote of 69 to 20 and all that remained was for a conference committee to insure the uniformity of the two measures.

The outcome was a remarkable tribute to the cohesive power of the NRECA. The response to Nixon's axe was swift and wisely directed to bring action at the earliest possible moment. The lesson for the future even as the co-ops grow bigger and more diversified is the vital need for co-op member participation and concern. As the Nixon shock proved, nothing either past or present can be taken for granted.

Given the size and importance of the rural electrics, it is hard to see how Nixon could have thought that his fiat would bring the program to a full stop. Basin Electric Power Cooperative with headquarters at Bismarck, North Dakota is an outstanding example of what co-operation means. Ingeniously built into a hillside so that it does not impede the sweep of the plain, the four-story headquarters building with one-third supplemental solar heating houses 400 staff and assistants. The scrupulously clean interiors hum with life presided over by James Grahl, Basin's manager, whose conspicuous attributes are modesty and compassion that go with quiet efficiency in presiding over a power system serving eight states with one million consumers in co-ops, public power systems and municipalities.

Size is not alone what gives Basin its unique status. It is an example of what a link between hydro and thermal power can mean. The development of hydro power on the great watersheds of America was one of the goals of the New Deal. The Tennessee Valley Authority had been established against the fierce opposition of the private power industry. A similar authority was projected for the Missouri and Columbia Rivers, but after years of wrangling the political opposition proved too strong. Nevertheless the six dams were built on the upper Missouri. Together with the Yellowtail dam on the Big Horn River in Montana, these dams produce 2,200,000 kilowatts of hydroelectric power.

The origin of Basin Electric goes back to a courageous advocate of hydro power. In the ten years he served on the Federal Power Commission, five years as chairman, Leland Olds was an unfailing proponent for the consumer and for preference power to co-op and municipal users from the dams already built. Not surprisingly this won him the enmity of the powerful oil and natural gas interests the commission was supposed to regulate. That quickly became evident when President Truman in 1949 nominated him for a third term on the commission. The oil and gas lobbyists dug up articles which Olds had written twenty or more years before and tried to pin the communist label on him. The nomination was bottled up in committee for months, and finally Truman went into action calling on widespread support to move the Olds name onto the Senate floor. There the Senate voted to reject the nomination 53 to 15. The outcome was ascribed to the oil and gas lobby, with key Senators the target.

For Olds, working with various organizations outside government, this was the beginning of a crusade for low-cost hydro power that would benefit consumer co-ops and municipally owned systems. In an historic address at the Midwest Electric Consumers Association meeting in Rapid City, South Dakota, on October 26, 1959, he gave inspiration for a coordinated power system in the eight states of the Missouri Basin. It was a carefully detailed paper reflecting all of Olds' knowledge of power and the relationship between investor owned power rates and the role of rural electric cooperatives.

"You should put yourself in position as a group to deal from strength rather than as a large number of separate entities, from weakness," he began by saying. "Remember that the secret of giant power doesn't lie simply in a maze of contractual arrangements under a dozen separate rate schedules making it possible to build individual generating stations that are larger and more efficient than a single system alone could build. The secret lies, rather, in establishing a single regional wholesale power supply system that can build and integrate such giant plants as a source of bulk power supply for all systems in the region. Only through separating the power supply function from the distribution function can the business of electric service be put on a sound basis."

Olds pointed to the strength that already existed in consumer power development in the eight states as shown on the masthead of the Midwest Electric Consumers Association. There were 850 public and co-operative systems serving more than one-and-a-half million consumers, more than 40 per cent of all the electric users in the region. Besides Nebraska with its 100 per cent public power supply, the seven other states included 13 operating generating and transmission co-operatives that were already delivering wholesale power to 149 rural electric co-ops as well as supplying many small municipal systems. At the same time twelve municipal systems were supplying power to co-ops. In the eight states public and co-op power was already a 10 billion kwh a year business.

This would seem in itself a sufficient development. But Olds left no doubt that the temper of the Republican administration was to leave regional power supply planning to the private power companies operating through their own interconnected systems. In other words, after absorption of Federal Bureau of Reclamation power small public and co-op electric systems would return to their position on the purchasing end of a monopoly system. That was why it was absolutely essential to form a unified system capable of building the largest generating stations at the best possible sites for integrated operation with federal hydroelectric power.

That was the goal as defined by Olds. Pulling together all the elements took years of study, preparation and often contentious debate by representatives of generation, transmission and distribution co-ops. The Basin Electric Power Cooperative was incorporated on May 5, 1961, its goal was the development of large-scale economical generating plants to meet the future power supply needs of its preference customers in the Upper Missouri Basin.

Construction was begun on the first steam generating plant at Stanton, North Dakota. Fittingly it was called Leland Olds after the prime mover who had had the practical vision to see what an integrated power system could mean. Integrated with "peaking" power from the Missouri River dams Olds Unit No. 1, and construction in the early '70s of Unit No. 2, the power supply was sufficient to meet the growing needs of the region.

The great advantage of the steam generating plants was the proximity of low-cost lignite. Efficiency in burning lignite, also known as brown coal, was rated at the Olds units higher than anywhere else in this country. Having been late in developing, the power needs of the region quickly expanded and so did Basin's operation. The William J. Neal plant at Velva, North Dakota was acquired and 7200 miles of high voltage transmission lines were built in a pooling agreement with the Bureau of Reclamation. Basin built as part of the agreement two 345 kilovolt lines spanning 526 miles from the Olds station to Bureau of Reclamation substations at Watertown and Fort Thompson, South Dakota. This meant that Unit 2 power was fed into the regional transmission grid.

Given Basin's size it is a continuing effort to hold the interest of perhaps a million consumers who are in one degree or another also co-operators. It is not a big business but an endeavor sustained by thousands of men and women throughout the region who give their time and effort to Basin. A key figure in holding this interest is Win Curtiss, manager of information. To save time where scheduled service is scarce or nonexistent Curtiss in speaking to co-ops around the region frequently uses small charter planes as do other Basin executives. Dropping down out of the sky gives a touch of drama to Curtiss' appearance and the speech he makes with his special brand of humor and earnestness on the role of the co-operator. Dedicated members of the board give unstintingly of their time to directing a far-flung co-operative enterprise with board meetings each month at Bismarck. Bob Valen puts in twelve-hour days as coordinator of impact planning insuring that strip-mined land is restored.

Basin Electric with its pioneering power plants and innovative direction at every level could not have come about without a long struggle over the right of co-operatives to generate and distribute their own power when there was a fundamental need. Basin came as the climax of that struggle; it was proof of the power of co-operators when an administration in Washington understood the role of rural America in the power equation.

The major battle was over the Indiana Statewide Rural Electric Co-operative. It began in 1961 when REA made a loan to Indiana Statewide's Hoosier Energy Division of $100.4 million for a generating and transmission system to serve 16 rural electric co-ops with more than 380,000 farm and other consumers in 44 Indiana counties. REA Administrator Norman M. Clapp found that generating and transmission were essential if the Hoosier co-ops were to get power at a fair cost. Clapp had the strong support of President John F. Kennedy who proved to be the staunchest presidential advocate of rural power.

The private utilities led by Public Service of Indiana immediately went to court to try to prevent construction of the G and T. When that failed the next move was to try to enjoin Hoosier from selling power to consumers. Construction went steadily on. But in 1969 in response to a suit brought by the Southern Indiana Gas & Electric Company the state supreme court of Indiana by a majority of three to two held that the right of Hoosier's parent, Indiana Statewide EC, to operate G and T facilities under Indiana's Rural Electric Membership Corporation Act of 1935 had lapsed because of failure to use it earlier. Clapp quickly took a bold move to insure that so much of the future of REA in power resources would not be brought to a full stop. Eighteen days after the decision of the Indiana court, in an agreement between REA and Hoosier, the United States government took control of Hoosier's facilities. An unprecedented move, it had the backing of Secretary of Agriculture Orville Freeman. An attempt by investor owned utilities to get the Supreme Court of the United States to intervene failed.

Clapp had scored a great triumph in upholding the integrity of the generating project. All during the long obstructionist siege building had gone on with $75 million of the loan drawn on. The efforts of Public Service of Indiana to stymie Hoosier did not end with the federal takeover. A federal judge was found who would enjoin Hoosier from operating. A new administration had come into being with little interest in breaking this stalemate.

But the initial victory was more important than the fate of the Hoosier project. Clapp, perhaps the boldest and most innovative REA administrator, had established what came to be known as the third criterion for the loan program. It was not enough to make sure farmers and ranchers however remote from power lines should be served. Nor was it enough to restrict loans to the distribution of power from whatever source might be available. In announcing a loan to the Alabama Electric Cooperative for generating and transmission Clapp spelled out as follows what was to be known as the third criterion:

"Both the present relationship and possible future conflicts of interest must be considered in the light of a long history of friction and hostility between the Alabama Power Company and the co-operative electric systems in Alabama. Under these circumstances the future security and effectiveness of the co-operative rural electric systems require a source of power completely dedicated to their interests."

This was the policy Clapp followed during his eight years as administrator with the full backing of Presidents Kennedy and Johnson. It is the reason the co-ops have made an important contribution to the nation's total supply of energy. The growth of the G and Ts has been phenomenal. A recent list of the 55 co-ops with generating and transmission facilities shows that they generate a total of 11,117.39 megawatts with 43,697 miles of transmission serving 693 distribution co-ops. In the first 20 years of the program, power supply capital requirements were only 25 per cent of the total. This went to 50 per cent in the 1960s and to 80 per cent of loan funds in 1979. It is estimated that by the year 2000 rural electric systems will be providing 16 per cent of all power delivered to consumers. That will mean investment of billions of dollars, much of it coming from commercial sources.

But dollars and kilowatt hours are only one measure of the growth of a remarkable institution. Human participation and human interest, human quirks and human ingenuity are another measure. Nowhere is this more evident than in New Mexico where the geographic spread of the 17 co-ops covers the state, and for one of the most sparsely populated states in the Union this is no small achievement. It owes a lot to Carl M. Turner who for years has been statewide manager.

Turner has a deep long-standing knowledge of the politics of his state which, combining three ethnic strains—Indian, Mexician-American and Spanish—are often far from the conventional norm. From his comfortable headquarters, a converted residence in Santa Fe, he keeps a knowing eye on the state legislature. Riding with Turner through the beautiful mountain country around Taos served by the Kit Carson Electric Co-operative, is to share his easy humor and his intimate knowledge of the varying peoples who earn their keep in this rugged terrain. He likes to tell the story of the five millionth farm family hooked up as a result of REA electric loans to the Lea County Electric Co-operative at Lovington in 1962. With a sense of what this would mean he arranged for the housewife, Mrs. Margaret McGuffin, to talk on her new telephone over a direct line with Secretary of Agriculture Orville Freeman in Washington. The family got telephone service the same day from Leaco Rural Telephone Co-operative. With a loud speaker set up to broadcast their talk, a thousand or more friends and fellow co-operators were gathered for the great occasion. Norman Clapp had come out from Washington. But a neighboring housewife chose that moment to try out her new telephone; the radical transformation of a lonely ranch house both in light and communication. The ensuing conversation—husbands, pigs, chickens, children—was duly broadcast with the star of the occasion too polite and too bemused to hang up on her friend. But Secretary Freeman had patiently stood by, and the historic exchange with Mrs. McGuffin was duly sent out if not to the world at least to a large part of New Mexico.

Kit Carson Electric Co-operative is benefiting from two large-scale consumers on the co-op lines. One is the Molybdenum Corporation mine which is being greatly enlarged. When the expansion of the mine, a subsidiary of the Union Oil Company, is completed revenue to Kit Carson is estimated at $1 million a month. The other consumer is a large resort area, Angel Fire, with ski lifts, tennis courts, a golf course, condominiums and handsome vacation houses, largely financed by Texas capital. The revenue from Angel Fire when it is completed is put at $50,000 annually. The co-op directors point out what this will mean toward leveling rates to farmer-rancher co-operators served in many instances on lines strung across the mountains with only one or two consumers to a mile. The average income of co-op members is $6000 a year. The issue of the right to supply a large-scale consumer was fought out in 1972 in the Columbus Electric Co-operative at Deming when by a vote of four to one members voted to reject sale to an investor owned utility and to supply power to the Phelps Dodge mining operation. The vote for keeping the co-op was taken despite the fact that their rate was nearly twice as high as that of the Public Service Company of New Mexico.

As everywhere in the country power needs grow with irresistible pressure. The Plains G & T Co-operative at Albuquerque has applied for a loan of $300 million for a coal-fired generating plant to supply eleven co-op members with 50 megawatts of power. As an evidence of the inroads of inflation the plant would have cost $38 million 25 years ago. Wholesale power rates from Plains eight years ago were nine mills. The rate now is three cents and in three years it will go to five cents. That makes it abundantly clear why Kit Carson, for example, feels it benefits its consumers to serve large-scale users in its service area.

The mounting cost of meeting environmental impact requirements adds to the power bill around the country, and the co-ops try scrupulously to meet these requirements. Of the $300 million loan to Plains perhaps as much as $100 million will go for impact alleviation. A striking example cited by co-operative leaders is the obstacle course that had to be crossed before construction was authorized of the $1.6 billion Laramie River power station to serve six consumer owned utilities as part of the Missouri Basin Power Project. Federal, state and local agencies had requirements for water, land and air use calling for 43 separate permits. And after all permits had been granted and construction well under way, further hurdles were put up following an injunction by a federal judge in Omaha. The need for a resting—not nesting—place for the whooping cranes on their migration from Texas to Canada was met with a trust fund of $7½ million to be drawn on to save the sand bars where some 75 cranes might rest when they interrupt their flight.

Size does not inhibit experimentation. The Lea County co-op has just been given a $3 million grant from the Department of Energy for a new experimental form of solar heating. Known as photovoltaic, the panels convert sunlight directly into electric power. This is then converted into the voltage used by the co-op throughout its distribution system. The photovoltaic system will supply 20 per cent of the power for a shopping center near Lovington, and since the system does not store power the co-op will supply the balance from conventional sources. K. C. Martin, general manager of the Lea co-op, with its 5500 members, believes all possible sources of energy should be tried out. We are an energy co-operative, he says, as he considers the use of windmills, one of 10 kilowatts, another of 40 kilowatts, the average price $500 per kw. At the same time he believes that conservation is essential.

A bold advocate of experimentation is Wally Beyer, the aggressive general manager of the Verendrye Electric Co-operative at Velva, North Dakota. The co-op is working with two private firms to use sunflower seed as a source of heat to generate power in a project with a loan guarantee of $25 million from the Farmers Home Administration. Sunflowers are an important crop in the plains country, and in the past they have been shipped outside the state to processing plants in this country and abroad. The transportation cost has reduced the return to the farmer. Under the plan, steam from Basin Electric's Neal plant which is six miles from Velva would be used to process the oil from 1500 tons of seed a day. Up to 100 tons of hulls a day would be burned in the Neal plant boilers along with lignite to generate power for the system. It has taken a lot of dickering, with Beyer as the catalyst, to move this proposal along.

Beyer is also a strong advocate of conservation as a member of NRECA's Energy Conservation Committee. As he put it in a talk to the annual co-op meeting, the choice is not conservation or consumption but conservation and consumption. Without sacrificing standards, every means should be taken to get the most power out of every dollar spent. Home heating with electricity has taken hold in recent years, and given North Dakota's winters the bill for heating 1100 square feet in an average house can run from $400 to $500 a month. With the resources of Verendrye, Beyer is encouraging home insulation, showing co-operators how to take advantage of various forms of public help. As power rates threaten to double in the 1980s he is proud of a turnout of 1400 to 1500 for an annual meeting to hear the good and the bad news. The membership is 6700.

Chapter Fifteen

BROADENING HORIZONS

THE broad sweep of America and the striking range of climate and way of life from one region to another is shown in the variations of the rural co-ops. They are not merely branch operations following the pattern of a centralized bureaucracy. Within the common scope of serving farms and rural communities with low cost power they have different methods, different aspirations. And nowhere is this more apparent than in the Pacific Northwest which can lay claim to being the birthplace of the public power movement and where the co-ops were to play an important role.

The origins go back to the beginnings of public power in cities such as Takoma where as early as 1893 the mutuals provided electricity for city consumers. The Minidoka Irrigation project around Burley, Idaho was another example of people working together to provide their own power needs. This was a forerunner of the great power project that harnessed the Columbia River during the New Deal. One of the far-sighted prophets of the development that was to transform the Northwest was Senator Homer T. Bone of Washington. He led the fight to allow the Takoma mutuals to sell power to the co-ops outside the city, winning after a long struggle with the investor owned utilities. Bone drafted the bill creating public utility districts with the result that 75 per cent of all power in the state of Washington is public.

His long view was evident in the Senate when in 1933 he put his weight behind the creation of the Tennessee Valley Authority with a preference clause for public users. This was the forerunner of Bonneville and Grand Coulee which were started that same year. Today there are 30 dams on the Columbia, and the power grid extends from southernmost California to Canada thanks to a treaty with Canada providing for the link up. This has cut the annual destructive flood on the Columbia by half. The wealth of power over and above that going to preference customers has meant industries such as aircraft, aluminum and electronics developing at so rapid a rate that any downturn in the economy will be felt less in the Northwest than anywhere else in the country. But as the need for power began to outstrip available resources, the administrator of the Bonneville Power Administration, Sterling Munro, confronted demands for increased energy from all BPA's customers. Speaking to the Northwest Public Power Association he gave this reassurance:

"The power business in the Northwest has been admired by outsiders as a remarkable blend of co-operating utilities and agencies. No part of this blend has solely dominated the region. But together we have been able to build an efficient integrated regional power system. And the most important single relationship for BPA has been with its preference customers."

The co-ops have grown faster than any other element. Since 1951 they have increased from 33 to 54. Their use of power during the same period increased from 333 million kwhs to 6.492 billion kwhs. Because of continuing conflict with investor owned utilities, the growth of the co-ops in Oregon has not been as rapid as elsewhere. Out of this situation a new relationship has developed with the IOUs. The co-ops have shown that they are not hesitant to do business with the IOUs, and for their part the IOUs welcome the capital that can come by way of the REA co-ops.

The best example is the Pacific Northwest Generating and Transmission Co-op made up of 17 distributing co-op members. General Manager David E. Piper has negotiated a remarkable deal with the Portland General Electric Company. For $70,000,000 Pacific Northwest has acquired ten per cent, 53,000 kwhs, of the power from the company's Boardman coal-fired plant. Since the co-ops will get preference power from Bonneville until BPA in July of 1983 files a notice of insufficiency, the power from Boardman which goes on the line in July 1980 will not be needed. So Pacific Northwest is selling back the power to Portland General Electric for the three-year period. The cost is 43 mills per kwh, and BPA will wheel the power. In some respects a unique arrangement, it would have been inconceivable a decade ago. Portland General will have 80 per cent of the output from Boardman, Idaho Power and Light ten per cent, and the Pacific Northwest co-op ten per cent.

It is a long way from that kind of sophistication to the northern-most electric co-op in Barrow, Alaska. Like most of the co-ops which have gained wide acceptance in the far north state, the Barrow Electric Utilities Co-operative performs many services for its members. Like other institutions that have come into being, the co-op is trying to bridge the past, the hunter in the frozen sea, the igloo, the fur trader, and the present, the native claims act, prosperity spilling over from Prudhoe Bay, and the snowmobile with gasoline at $3 a gallon. Today there are 14 co-ops in the state with the Alaska Village Co-operative, the most remarkable, serving 48 separate Eskimo communities. Although Alaska Village can reach its members only by plane, the magic of power has made it a bustling community with that magic reaching out to communities, some with only a few hundred consumer members. Since more than 90 per cent of power comes from oil-fired diesel generators, power rates are high. While only nine per cent is from hydro, co-op leaders look longingly at the many untapped rivers that are jealously guarded by environmentalists.

A sympathetic treatment of Alaska in transition was in *Ruralite*, an outstanding magazine among the many excellent publications put out by statewide associations around the country. *Ruralite* serves 45 co-ops and public utility districts in Oregon, Washington, Nevada and Alaska with a circulation of 175,000. The magazine is exceptional in providing for each individual co-op and PUD subscriber and their membership a special section devoted to the concerns of that particular area. In short, within the frame of broader interests, it is a regional magazine. Ken Dollinger, the energetic editor, presides in a modern new building in Forest Grove, Oregon, which is next door to the printer. It follows that Gus Norwood, who might well be called Mr. Public Power having served on the Northwest Public Power Association, spent five years in Alaska as head of Alaska's federal power agency and is now historian of BPA, is an influential member of *Ruralite's* publications board. He has been part of the history of the co-ops, knowing their struggles when farms consolidated, when the small stump ranchers pulled up stakes, and when the small "gippo" loggers disappeared. The story is a part of the mighty current that flows out of the Columbia; a force transforming a vast region and even though the problems of supply and demand are today acute, it cannot be doubted that they will be resolved.

It would be hard to think of a greater contrast than the Lumbee River Electric Membership Corporation covering four counties in eastern North Carolina with headquarters in Red Springs. Lumbee River has gone through great difficulties in the past, one being conflict over the ethnic balance as between Lumbee Indians, blacks and whites in the top direction of the co-op. As this was worked out, with the intensive activity of the Indians and their acute ethnic consciousness, there are today ten Indians on the twelve-man board of directors, one white and one black. The chairman of the board, Elias Rogers, is a Lumbee.

While this did not solve the basic problem which is related to the low income level of Robeson County, the lowest of any county in the state, the co-op is moving to help members resolve their problems. It is an outstanding example of the kind of service a co-operative can give beyond merely supplying power and sending out bills. To hold the loyalty and the interest of members as power rates go up—this is the function that co-ops everywhere are going to have to perform.

With a new rate jump, members were increasingly unable to meet their monthly bills. They were often the elderly living on small social security checks. The routine would have been a $10 charge for delinquent payment and if the bill still was not paid the power would be cut off. For Manager Derl Hinson and Services Manager John O'Briant that was self-defeating. Under the direction of Genevieve Edens, a long-time employee of Lumbee with a thorough knowledge of the whole area, and with the help of three person-to-person representatives, a program was initiated to galvanize the resources of the social service agencies in Red Springs and the nearby towns. Electric bills could not be paid out of the funds of these public or semi-public agencies, but the funds could provide various forms of assistance that most members were not aware of. So now when an unhappy member unable to pay the monthly bill comes in or writes or manages to phone on what has become known as the hot line, the process begins of finding help from federal, state and private sources. It is a slow process and the help is far from munificent, but the prospect is that in most instances it will supply a margin of extra income making it possible to pay electric bills. In other ways, too, Lumbee is helping members. Low interest loans through the co-op for home weatherization and a load management program to reduce the peak demand for electricity are actively pursued.

A tour of the region with Ronnie Hunt, Manager of Staff Services, leaves no doubt of the problems of poverty in a time of rapid change. From the era not long ago of a team of mules and a patch of cotton, tenant farmers almost all, tobacco the cash crop, massive tractors and earth-moving machines are taking over. Along the roads are the tenant houses of the past, many abandoned and falling into ruin, those who can still work finding farm jobs in the season and perhaps employment at new small industries coming into the region. These are proud people often reluctant to accept help that seems to be charity. The Lumbee Indians are themselves a remarkable heritage having survived with sharp awareness of their own identity without any separate cultural background or tribal cohesion other than the legend that they are the descendants of the "lost tribe" going back to the sixteenth century.

Important developments are just ahead. Lumbee River and 26 of North Carolina's 28 co-ops have signed up for the initial administrative costs for a statewide network that will build a thermal plant using North Carolina's plentiful supply of peat along with 48-year contracts when the plant is built. If in a period of transition the co-operative can be a kind of bridge between past and present it will have given the members a sense of owning a stake in their future. And since it has proved increasingly difficult to get members out for the annual meeting, plans are going forward for small group sessions to discuss the details of Lumbee's operation.

Forrest F. (Bud) Stacy can stand as the model of the new co-operative man; a portent of the future. At 38, spare, compact, giving off vibes of energy, he is general manager of the Oglethorpe Power Corporation that in five years has become the tenth largest wholesaler of electricity in the nation in terms of square miles served. Oglethorpe and Stacy speak for a radical change in the approach to rural electrification. Much of the story in *The Farmer*

Takes a Hand details the confrontation between co-ops as they developed and expanded and investor owned utilities. In Georgia cooperation and not confrontation is the order of the day. With the confidence he radiates Stacy believes this is the pattern of tomorrow.

Georgia may have been a special case although Stacy does not think it was all that different from the condition prevailing elsewhere. Until the formation of Oglethorpe on August 8, 1974, the principal wholesale supplier for the 39 distribution co-ops throughout the state was the Georgia Power Company. For two or three years beginning in 1972 the company was in trouble, with difficulty raising capital for investment to meet the projected needs for sizable new energy demands.

At this point Oglethorpe, having been formed by the 39 statewide co-ops, came along with a bundle of cash in the form of loans from the Federal Financing Bank guaranteed by REA. This was just what Georgia Power needed and from that point on under the leadership of Stacy and his board of directors and Robert Scherer, president of Georgia Power, events moved swiftly. Oglethorpe invested $182 million in an integrated transmission system tying in power from private and public distributors. With nuclear power considered an indispensable factor in meeting projected power needs, Oglethorpe invested $323 million in Georgia Power's Hatch nuclear plant then in operation. Another commitment of $107 million went to the Vogtle nuclear plant under construction, and for a future purchase in Vogtle a whopping $681 million. Advances already made and commitments for the future add up to $2.116 billion.

Working closely on a friendly basis with Scherer of Georgia Power, Stacy believes that with the end of the era of confrontation there has been an end, too, to the investor owned propaganda that the co-ops are socialist or communist. Although this may emanate in the lower and middle sectors of private industry, it is no longer the dominant theme at the top and that is the more remarkable since Oglethorpe and the co-ops compete actively for sales to private industry even though the industrial plant may not be on a co-op line. As diagrammed by Stacy it works like this: Oglethorpe provides the expertise with the detail and efficiency that have been its hallmark. Armed with this material, the local member makes the bid to the private plant in its area with a load demand above 900 kilowatts. In competition with the private supplier, member co-ops have obtained 80 to 85 per cent of these contracts. Some of these are big such as when the Southern Paper Company doubled its load capacity and Altamaha Electric Membership Corporation got the contract.

What is the difference, it may well be asked, between Oglethorpe and an investor owned utility particularly since in 1979 the name was changed from Oglethorpe Electric Membership Corporation to

Oglethorpe Power Corporation. This was done "to better define its operation and to avoid possible confusion with the responsibilities of a distribution co-operative." Stacy dismisses this question as irrelevant. He points to the high degree of Oglethorpe's efforts devoted to serving the 39 electric membership corporations, the designation of the co-ops in Georgia, with four service divisions specializing in every aspect of economic and social development of the EMCs. It is the kind of efficiency that a large successful business might have. For example, Oglethorpe's proposal to add 100 to 150 employees and lease two floors in an adjoining building has been so thorough to demonstrate the need with charts, graphs and statistics as to fill a folder two inches thick for the members of the board.

The 39 board members may not all read this compilation, but it is there if they want to take the time. Oglethorpe sold $29 million in pollution control bonds to finance pollution abatement facilities at the Hatch plant and at the Wansley thermal plant in which Oglethorpe has a stake of $159 million. All this is aimed at generation sufficiency for the 1990s with an amazing growth rate of 8.8 per cent a year. It anticipates, too, the certain jump in power rates. In 1970 the Oglethorpe rate was two cents a kwh. That went to a wholesale rate of three cents in November of 1979, with the distribution EMCs charging an average of 4.3 cents. An important factor in the cost of power is the soaring rate of interest. The average for Oglethorpe loans now outstanding is eight per cent, but that is sure to rise as more loans are drawn on.

A break came from the Georgia legislature passing an act assigning territorial integrity to the several suppliers. The map is like a patchwork quilt showing in red the 71 per cent of the state's land area served by Oglethorpe with more than 1,250,000 Georgians on its lines. The white areas in populous centers are those of Georgia Power. The blue are municipal electric systems; the green, a private utility out of Savannah; and on the northern boundary, in purple, EMCs served by TVA power. That, says Stacy, ended the squabbling. The map is reproduced in Oglethorpe's promotion literature.

If this is in fact the wave of the future it would astonish the founding fathers. They were ready for a standup fight for the right to serve the farthest outposts of rural America where there might be no more than two or three farmers or ranchers on a remote country line. That fight was often long delaying and expensive as in Indiana. The slogan today might be, need power, bring money. Stacy, who served a five-year apprenticeship with Iowa's five G and Ts, would not quibble with that.

The growing strength of the REA co-ops and their success in bringing light and power to rural America had begun to attract worldwide attention in the late '50s. Testifying in 1961 on the foreign aid program, co-operative leaders recommended the use of the co-operative method in the aid program. Events moved swiftly after that. When the NRECA board of directors met in June, General Manager Clyde Ellis urged them to go on record in support of the REA pattern and they unanimously passed a resolution instructing the staff to call attention of the appropriate agencies to the great potential of the co-ops in advancing international social and economic progress.

Before the inauguration Ellis had written to President-elect Kennedy telling him of the developments that included an amendment to the AID bill introduced by Hubert Humphrey calling it the declared policy of the government to encourage the use of co-operatives and credit unions in the foreign aid field. After lengthy organizing and planning sessions with representatives of NRECA and AID, a contract was ready to sign providing for the use of NRECA's services. President Kennedy, who from the beginning had been one of the staunchest supporters of REA, said that the contract was so important he wanted it signed by both parties on his desk in the White House. At the signing ceremony on November 1, 1962, Kennedy said:

"One of the most significant contributions that we can make to the under-developed countries is to pass on to them the techniques which we in this country have developed and used successfully. It seems to me, therefore, that the contract signed today holds special promise for those countries which have realized only a small fraction of their energy potential. I express the hope that the results of the contract will be an improved standard of living for millions of people."

With the creation of an International Programs Division in NRECA, funded by AID, the work began immediately with Dr. Thomas Venables in charge. Today advisory assistance and training have been provided to 36 countries, and more than 160 advisors representing 80 U.S. co-operatives plus specialists from REA and other organizations have taken part in 300 overseas assignments. The IPD staff, now headed by Samuel A. Bunker who had 15 years of experience with the Ford Foundation in Egypt and India before he joined NRECA, follows each new country that comes on line with excitement and anticipation as though for a son or daughter about to come of age.

The newest is Bangladesh. Under the leadership in the capital, Dacca, the concept of co-operatives to develop rural electrification was welcomed with enthusiasm. The goal was to do the whole job for 80,000,000 Bangladeshians. A feasibility study by International Programs concluded that this was too far too fast. Instead, it was decided to begin with 13 pilot co-ops. Members signing up have sometimes exceeded by three or four times the number essential to form a distribution co-op. Not only this but, in a country supposedly at the bottom of the poverty scale, they were bringing in the money to qualify as members. So hopeful is the development of the pilots that countrywide electrification is a practical goal. It is a joint project with Commonwealth Associates International which is planning the engineering while NRECA is the guide on the institutional side.

New nations are coming in fast. Representatives from countries planning electrification co-ops often come for IDP training institutes and then for two weeks visit co-ops around the country. Chullapongs Chulakesa from Thailand recently spent a few days at Lumbee River EMC. International Programs is working with the World Bank to develop electrification projects with a loan of $1.2 million for Yemen, $600,000 for Jamaica over a two-year period, and a $1.1 million for Egypt. These are, of course, initial stages that are expected to prepare the way for area-wide coverage. In each country light and power could be a transforming force.

The Philippines, beginning in 1962, is a conspicuous success. As much as half of the most highly cultivated land is now covered by 113 co-ops of which 85 to 90 are energized. The next stage is to carry electrification to poorer regions where hookups will be fewer and rates a problem. In some parts of the world, notably in Latin-America, central power authorities have retained the right of distribution. Far from doctrinaire, International Programs has given assistance to various agencies including co-ops when it has been called for.

Nothing could demonstrate more dramatically than this worldwide collaboration the authority of an idea whose time had come. As measured by astronomical time, the span from 1935 to today is hardly more than an eye wink. How gratifying it would be to the founding fathers of rural electrification to know that the outward thrust of their pioneering concept is bounded only by the dimensions of the globe itself. Franklin Roosevelt as prime mover had as inspiration and guide the Philadelphia engineer-financier Morris L. Cooke whose beliefs and abilities helped to shape the initial REA program. The founding fathers in Congress, Sam Rayburn and George Norris, and later others like Hubert Humphrey and George Aiken, were firm in their resolve to light up places so long dark. These are the pioneers to whom all honor is due.